Arboribus Musicorum

Trees of Music

Givnology Wellness Arts

Copyright © 2024

Givnology Wellness Arts

Creative Commons CC BY-SA includes the following elements:

BY: credit must be given to the creator.

SA: Adaptations must be shared under the same terms.

This license enables reusers to distribute, remix, adapt, and build upon the material in any medium or format, so long as attribution is given to the creator. The license allows for commercial use.

If you remix, adapt, or build upon the material, you must license the modified material under identical terms.

ISBN: 9780987871077

To those who uphold traditions and keep cultures and musics of the people alive and vibrant

Creative Commons CC BY-SA.

Givnology Wellness Arts
ARBORIBUS MUSICORUM, *Trees of Music*

p. cm.
Clever soft latin jazz soul cultural fusion original songs scores by a gifted composer-arranger and excellent keyboardist-pianist.
ISBN-13: **978-0987871077** (hbk.)
1. Musical Cultural Anthropology 2. Culture Crossing / Trans-Culturalism 3. Multicultural Philosophy 4. Ethnomusicology 5. Latin Jazz 6. Soul Music 7. Salsa Music 8. Original Music Songbooks 9. Music Theory 10. Music Instruction: Heuristics
 I. Title.
2024

Books › History › World › Civilization & Culture
Books › Arts & Photography › Music › Reference
Books › Arts & Photography › Music › Theory, Composition & Performance › Appreciation

Vincent of Givnology Wellness Arts is a technical writer & composer from California. He continues composing, arranging, writing, creating Education & Wellness New-Media.

Vincent's sheet music scores are clear, concise arrangements for pianists, keyboardists, guitarists, percussionists, soloists and vocalists. **To assist performing ensembles there are extra opportunities in the scores:** Scores for two hands of piano usually can play full parts on two keyboard or a split keyboard with piano and violin for example.

Standard chords are included for guitarists or any other accompanist to use and help performers understand song structure and chord progressions. Some songs have easy guitar fret-boards, and **most guitar chords have been simplified for beginners**.

Thanks George *"Thurgopedia"* Thurgood @RCM for academic excellence, expert teaching skills & creative collaboration.

Our Charmony Series:
1) Honoring Those That Went Before, Classical and World Music Piano Scores. 2) World Music Class, The Aspire Higher Project. 3) Vincent Trio Scores. 4) Soul + Salsa = Soulsa. 5) Barry's Songs I. 6) How To Be In Harmony.

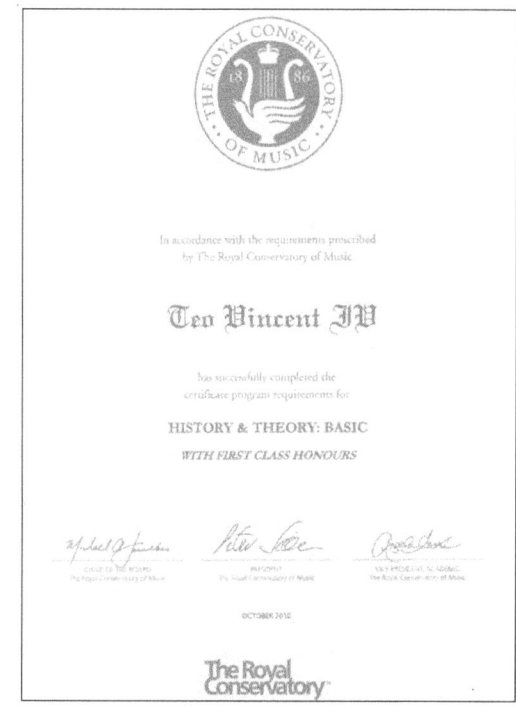

Givnology Wellness Arts
ARBORIBUS MUSICORUM, *Trees of Music*
ISBN-13: 978-0987871077

Books › History › World › Civilization & Culture
Books › Arts & Photography › Music › Reference
Books › Arts & Photography › Music › Theory, Composition & Performance › Appreciation

© 2024 Givnology Wellness Arts

Visit http://givnology.ca **for the latest files**

CONTENTS

Foreword:	vi
Part I	**1**
Seeds:	1
Branches:	2
Trees	3
Roots & Routes	6
Part II: Researches & References	**7**
Art Timeline	8
Selected Music Styles at the Turn of the 20th Century	13
History II Glossary	14
Great Composers	25
Musicionary	27
Non-Chord-Notes	29
Circle a non-chord note and specify using LABEL:	29
Ice-Cream-Chords	29
SetLists (sharing useful "Musical Shorthand")	30
Some of Vincent's Latest CD Inserts' Liner Notes	33
Vincent's "JamBase" FileMaker Song Database	37
Greek Modes or Scales	39
Part III: Latin Music Percussion Diagrams:	**39**
Percussionist Roles: Instruments' names are their roles	41
Clavitos, Claves For Beginners	42
Rumba	42
Montuno	42
Percs1: Da-dada-da-da	43
Percs2: Clave Down!	43
Percs3: Son Clave + Pulse	44
Percs4: Palito (Simple and Basic)	44
Percs5: Clave & Palito in Binary (back and forth)	45
Percs6: Rumba Clave, Palito & Binary	45
Percs7: Rumba Palito	46
Percs8: Rumba Clave & Rumba Palito in Binary	46
Percs9: Rumba Palito in 2-3 and Conga Dance	47
Percs10: 6/8 Agogo & Cowbell Patterns	47
Syncopated Agogo Pattern	47
Percs20: Entries – "Counting In" With Sides	48
Percs21: Endings – Outtros in Unison	48
Percs22: Hearing Songs' Claves & Sides	49
World Music Stories	49
Percussion Patterns Made into Melodic Phrases	49
Clave Offenders	50
Part IV	**51**
World Music Mastery, Building Blocks for Playing With Anyone!	51
World Music Definitions of Afro-Latin Music Percussion Roles & Rules	52
Complimenting Ensembles	59
Highlife has: 1-Rhythm, 2-Line and 3-Lead Guitar Parts	59
One Bar Calypso Percussion	60
Two Bar Soca (Soul-Calypso) Percussions	61
Rhythm Section Accompaniment "Chucks"	61
The Yoruba People from Nigeria, West Africa	62
Some Afro-Latin Music definitions:	62
Motifs and Motivations	63
Call and Response / Rhythmic Balance in Latin Music	63
Afro-American Contributions	63

All About The Bass 64
Perpetual Motivations 65
Syncro-Nice Sacred Rhythm Scales 66
    Conversation Pieces Solo: 1) Chords arpeggiated 2) Scales 3) Chromatic 67
The Montuno is a Great Motorvator 67
TIGHT SCHOOL 70
    Review: The Correct Side Of The Pattern 70
    Tres Golpes (3 gulps or 3 pulses) 70
CHUCKS (Accompaniment Accenting One or the Other Side) 72
DESIGNING MONTUNOS 72
Calypso Guitar Chucks 73
Sections, Unions & Oppositions 74
Louisiana style **Second-Line** chants calls and answers 74
Phrases 75
High Life Phrasing 75
When you can use Motorvations: 78
    Motives, motifs and motivational inspiring 78
Giving credit 78
Yradier's - Bizet's - Carmen's Habanera 79
Affirmatinas – Positive Message Music 79
Part V: More of Vincent's Original Scores **82**
Part VI: More of Vincent's Classical Reductions and Arrangements **115**
Bibliography 124
About The Author 127

Table of Scores

Vincent's 6 note blues scale with fingering which works great in C, D, E, G & A. 1
Montuno Etude #0, "Montuno Makes Blues Scale," Shekere pattern as Piano Montuno 50
Latin Piano (Montuno) 101: "La Bamba" 52
"Yoruba Diasporas" Rumba Parts translated into Melodic Phrases 54
Calypso Study in Soca (Soul-Calypso) often the first side (bar) is Up and the second half is Down 60
Chords in Brazilian Rimshot-Clave is a great foundation for solos 64
Syncro-Nice Sacred Rhythm Scales, Major & Lydian Sync to Sacred West-African rhythms. Melodic Minor Song. 66
Conversation Pieces: Extremely Potent Repeatable Motivations 67
Montuno Etude #1, Primer for First Time (Latin Piano) Technique 68
Montuno Etude #2, "That Makes This Heaven" C (I-VI-ii-V) Montuno and Bajo Tumbau (Bass) 69
"Calypso Circles," Circles of fifths with Calypso chuck (downbeat on the first half version) 74
Clavinet Keyboard Score 1, "Soca Clav" Soul-Calypso standard chuck 76
Clavinet Keyboard Score 2, "Superclav" Super Clavinet Technique 77
Affirmatinas: "Everything's going, now and ever more!" "Having what I'm wanting, wanting what I'm having" 80
"Take Me Home" Soft Latin Jazz • Circle of Fifths to Home, the Tonic (ii-V-I) 84
"Jamming Lesson #1" Improv Study Outline. Chord fretboards so beginners can join. Chords simplified. 91
"Guitar Jam" in Mi (E) Dominant (E7) - Guitar & Bass scored 92
"My Fantasy" Slow Salsa Groove with over 12 sections (Solos, Mambos, etc.) 94
"Lilly's Song" Improvisation Study of Major-Minor-Dominant as **CM Fm G7** (or **G Alt**) 107
"Swing Montuno" Study, 6/8 Swing Jazz Rhythmic Tension added to the Montuno Melodic Role 108
"Culture Crossing" Vincent's Latin Fusion group in San Francisco (Page 5 Rumba parts creatively scored) 110

Manuel Maria Ponce (1882-1948) "Gavotta #1 in D" 115
Antonio Vivaldi (1678-1741) Chamber Concerto in D major, RV 93 {Nice Guitar Chords added} 116
Gioacchini Rossini (1792-1868) Air & Chorus "Dal tuo stellato soglio" From the Sacred Drama "Mosè in Egitto" ... 118
Johannes Brahms (1833-1897) Hungarian Dance #11 {Simplified} 120
Franz Joseph Haydn (1732-1809) Symphony #88 Largo {For big hands} 122
Niccolò Paganini (1782-1840) "Cantabile" 124

Foreword:

Music is like a giant tree. We are like little monkeys who live in it, who identify with it and maybe try to help it, but it is an eternal thing much larger than any of us.

My journey into music has been like a spiritual awakening. From my first song Soul-African-Study to the multicultural experiences documented in my Soulsa & now Classical periods; learning more about myself, my Self Actualization is sharing **Music Appreciation & Literacy** as much as I can.

My great-grandfather was Teo Vincent the first. His grandfather Joao Antonio Mendonca Vincent published the very first Portuguese language newspaper in the United States, "Journal de Noticias" from 1877 to 1884. No wonder I feel so at home sharing strange but beautiful symbols and articulations. Thank you Joao. I am glad to honor you and fulfill your intentions.

My music is my Musical Cultural Anthropology (or Ethno-Musicology) project. I was born and raised in California, from Los Angeles to the San Francisco Bay Area. It is a great melting-pot of culture! The music in my books is my way of documenting the culture I am from. The virtuoso and composer Frédéric François Chopin (1810 – 1849) created many songs in the Polonaise form, honoring Poland; my "Soulsa" music perhaps is my **"Californaise."**

I've been blessed to be inspired by so many lovely sounds: Soul Music, Caribbean, Spanish, African, Classical, Jazz, Fusion, Rhythm & Blues, Flamenco, Disco, Funk and many more. I am very glad to share with you some of these artistic styles and influences. *May they flow freely to you without me being in the way.*

Perhaps music is more alive than us. We might just be an organic growth that enjoy it and therefore have it around us, but in fact it might be that the music is intelligent, eternal, and simply allows us to think that we are in charge of things.

Ludwig van Beethoven is still alive. A Stradivarius violin today would have lived from the beginning of violin making, through the development of the piano, electronics, recordings and broadcasts and is still revered by many as the finest musical craftsmanship ever created by a human.

Since I found out in 2006 about my grandmother Claudia Ruddock-Vincent the concert pianist and her great grandfather Theodore Dehon Ruddock the music professor, I realize that I am just a channel, a vehicle. I acknowledge that I am just the current carrier of this tradition. It is an honor, but also humbling to know I am only a node or network point in the life of the music flowing through. May I not be in the way of my art. May I correctly assist fulfilling my ancestors' dreams and intentions.

Part I

Seeds:

They say: "Imitation is the highest form of flattery." So much of music is one person building on the last, someone taking it over from there, and when you see routes (and roots) it becomes even more fun! Nowadays people loop and sample, but real art is upholding the complex nuances of a loved form and keeping the difficult task of actually playing, performing music such that it gives respect and demands respect.

Most all white Rhythm & Blues & especially Blues artists will always give credit to the originators of that so loved genre. René Fleming the amazing Opera singer was asked: "Any singer can sing *SPIRITUALS,* right?" She answered to the effect that, no, we respect that form and mostly leave it to them to be it's voice.

There are so many obvious HIGHEST FORMS OF FLATTERY: Elvis' "Hound Dog" was Big Momma Thornton's big hit, many songs by The Beatles were Chuck Berry's, The ABCs is Baa Baa Black Sheep, Twinkle Twinkle Little Star & on & on!

There was a time that the great pianist & singer Little Richard was pulled from the microphone, silenced, while on a music awards show he was saying how the originators of many hit songs who couldn't copyright them because they were black would be sitting on a curb and the famous white people playing their music would just walk past them.

Dad & I would make a tape every year of music we played together, copy it and send it to the whole family. We would switch and play either guitar or piano.

My father was so proud of his huge old "78s" records! I was so inspired by Guitar Slim's "Story of my Life" and his wild ornaments, it sounded like he had guitar foot-pedal effects but he didn't, he was just that wild! I modified his technique into a Blues improvising technique that I can still play whenever I want to.

He took me to "As Is" a Jazz Club in Venice, California when I was obviously too young (15). You could hardly see through the smoke! I remember a happy pianist scoping out the harmonies then proudly playing 10 finger masterful chords!

Vincent's intense 6 note Blues Scale (with fingering which works great in C, D, E, G & A)

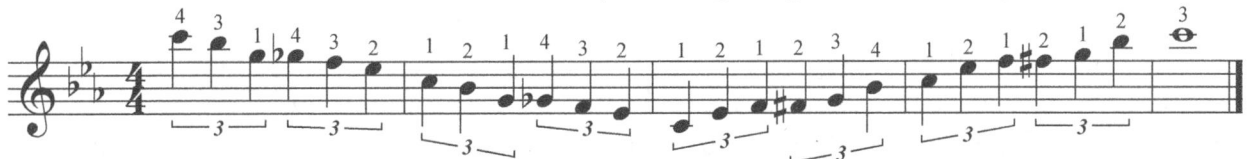

Hold down a low Eb (the "relative major") and the scale flips to a happy Carnival type feel!
On the subject of Musical Seeds and Imitation I usually say to people:

> *A guy in Cuba playing Latin Music is being a Spanish Guy and an African Guy. Sebastian Yradier, a Basque guy, brought Cuban music back to Spain by being a Cuban Guy. Georges Bizet (who never even went to Spain) borrowed the Carmen's Habanera melody from Yradier, being a Basque guy.*
>
> *Many musicians of all races & backgrounds consider Bizet's "Carmen" the definition of pure Gypsy style, and when they play it they are being a French guy!*

Music is all IMPERSONATION. On a Scott Yoo video a pianist said something like: "Here is how Beethoven would play this. Here is how Bach would. Handel would do it like this. Mozart like this.." It was such a delicious episode of "Now Hear This." In music, diverse cultures adding their own flair is such a treasure. ***Viva La Difference!***

When I was a Multi-Keyboardist with "Amandla Poets," an African Reggae band, I would quote themes from Funk music. On a song the leader would Rap in Causa language I would take synthesizer solos & get down on my knees like a guitarist. Patrick an arranger / bassist in the band had them all quote the jazzy section of Brides of Funkenstein's "The Mothership Connection Is Here" in my solo.

Branches:

West Indians have the benefit of their Indian heritage (like week long wedding parties) as well as the contributions of the black slaves that they mixed with. Some non-mixed Indians dislike them for that race mixing. West Indians know Indian culture, for example, Kali is the Hindu god of Marijuana that they call "Kali Herb." Reggae lyrics are perhaps the most peaceful and Universally uniting of all.

West Indians' premier invention is taking old filthy Oil Drums and inventing one of the most beautiful new instruments out of them: The Steel Drum.

In California & up the West Coast I performed a lot of Reggae, also did some Soca & Zouk. Some of the music is monotonous, repetitive, copies & covers, but some is truly moving, soulful and even enlightening! Trinis, from Trinidad & Tobago, love having the biggest loudest sound system & intense dance rhythms. They are a lot of fun & are often Carnival Contest Winners!

I was telling a top dean & teacher at The Royal Conservatory of Music about my book "World Music Class" and he thought about it and said to me: "Handel was the first World Music artist." I thought about it; Handel had studied with Buxtehude in Germany, like Bach, but then spent years in Italy, and eventually brought that super-sad Greek Tragedy type of Opera all the way to Britain, and when Opera was not so fashionable he delivered maybe the most famous Oratorio "Hallelujah" to The UK complete with it's many notes per syllable "Melisma" Ha-a-a-a-a-a-le-lu-u-u-u-le-lujah or something close to that. ☺ We English-speaking folks owe Georg Frederic Handel a big thanks for that! I think..

Speaking of **The Baroque Period,** when I started playing Domenico Scarlatti's 555 Keyboard Sonatas I used to think: "Was he inspired by Flamenco?" Later on, learning his father was the Master Opera Composer of Naples, Italy, meaning he was super-educated in composing, then that he spent 4 years in Andalucia before settling in Madrid, now I think he either 1) Invented it or 2) Predicted it! Flamencos owe Scarlatti a big thanks! PS I love his music and feel he is like a Bach but without the fierce dislike of the augmented second, meaning, he could use the Spanish Phrygian scale all he wished, however dissonant & unusual! **He has great blob chords too, almost a reinvention of what a chord is!**

https://practicapoetica.com/articles/american-music-history-chart/

Below is just a small subset, please go to the source ↑

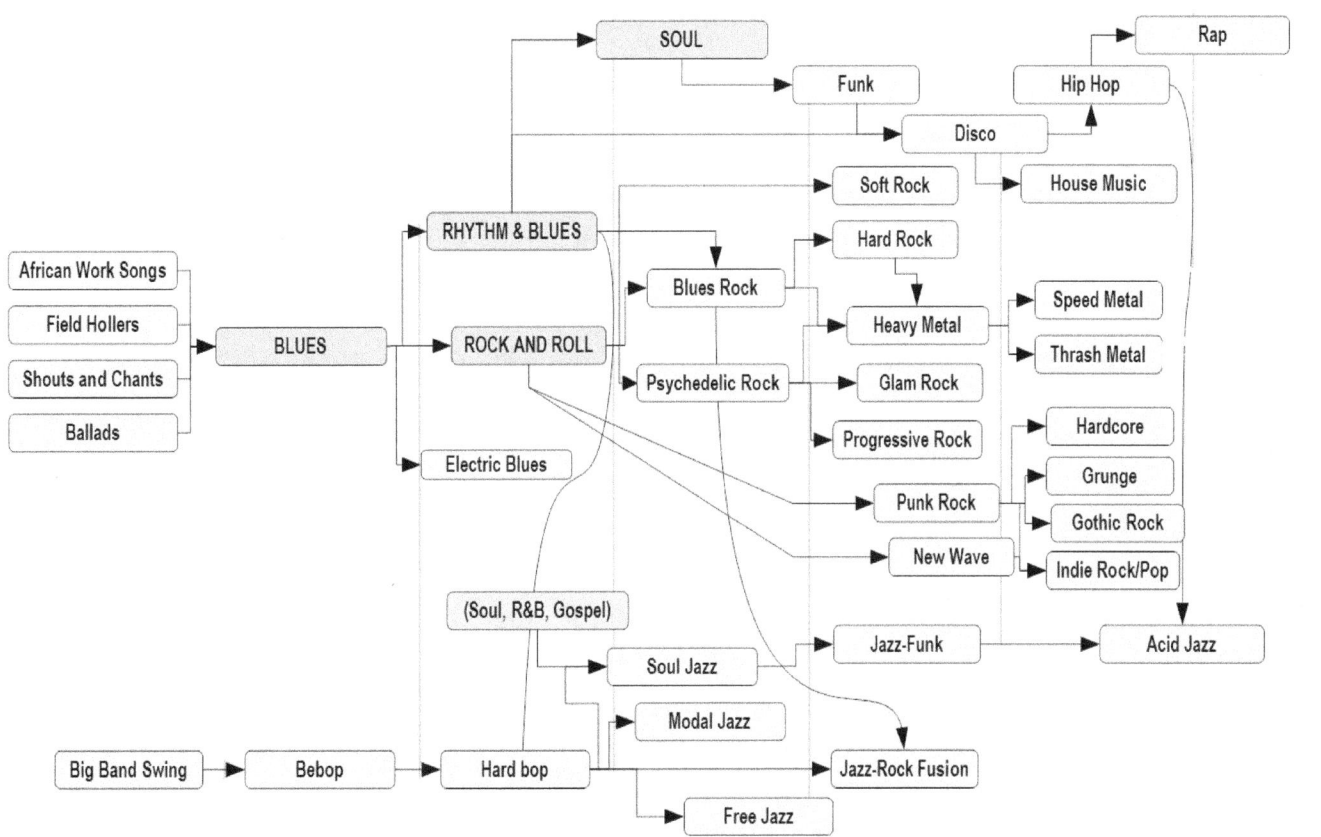

Trees

When I told a friend in California I was thinking of coming to Toronto to study Classical Music he said: "Well you can be the big fish in the little pond, or be the tiny fish in the big ocean." Yes he is right, I knew everyone in 6 or 7 music scenes, very well in California. I never had the opportunity to really study Classical & always wanted to. For a few years I thought: "OK 1 day I can add Classical to my list of styles I know." As I've learned the quantity and quality of the works, I realize now that Classical Music is larger than all the other musics I know, combined!

Beethoven is as large or larger than Salsa, Bach bigger than Jazz, shoot, his opus #s are over 1000! All singers use his SATB harmony rules, most instruments he has the standard sonatas to study, and he helped tune all the organs so we can play in any key! Mozart in his short 36 years composed so much music, today we would sue our boss & complain if they wanted that much work! Thanks Wolfgang!!!

My great RCM Jazz AND Classical teacher George Thurgood once said something that changed me forever: "Some of my best friends have been dead for hundreds of years." Probably because he saw my hunger to ever learn more and my admiration of Liszt, Chopin & so many other masters (he helped me with my scores of course). I feel humbled in Classical Music and wish I'd been perfecting my performance all my life continuously; trills getting better every year! I told Fred Perry my California KQED TV Producer boss and friend as a joke: "The ~Trill~ Is Gone!" To the theme of the Blues song "The Thrill Is Gone."

But one can always do their best and still learn great amounts with only OK trills. Once I told George a trill was difficult and he shouted at me: "Some Beethoven pieces you'll have 2 trills in 1 hand!" ☹ I do what I can.

Though I started Classical late in life, I think of Nureyev who started Ballet when many people quit (age 18). I also decided that the many years as a performer in many styles of music informs my own music knowledge that many pure Classical musicians wouldn't know about. They probably don't need to know some of what I know: improvising, turning Chopin into Salsa, flipping melodies & songs, rearranging & scoring for Guitar, Rhythm Section, Latin Arrangements & other things I know so <u>I'm OK being the little fish in the huge Classical Ocean.</u>

George & I discussed a very interesting composer who was also a teacher at the Royal Conservatory of Music, **Alexina Louie** who had some bizarre music notation where there were no bar lines, just times like 15 seconds, 30 seconds and the flags on notes increased as a graphic, not exact note divisions. But also, some of her music is wonderful! I saw violist James Ennis play a composition of hers and they even brought her onto the stage for standing ovations.

Talking about her George said: "Some composers, to avoid the fickle public, become academics and write things for each other; to show off advanced techniques. Sometimes they get so much into it that they forget the public altogether." This helped me value all the years of life experience collaborating with other artists in composing, arranging and performing. I have tons of funny gigging stories. **I'd say I have some strong** *Musical-Street-Smarts* ☺ !

Harry Best a wonderful and wonderfully mystic Steel Drummer in California shared a writing of his: "Rhythm and Spirit" where among other things he connected certain rhythmic patterns with the universal / cosmic trio: "+ − =" and making music math connections myself I came up with a completely unique technique: Playing the scale in the timing of the intervals. I knew I had found something important when I realized the Exon jingo uses this with "Exon we bring good things to life!" That's done in the major scale.

This is demonstrated in my scores: Syncro-Nice Sacred Music Scales. Why is this a Musical Tree not just a branch? Well I've developed many songs and studies playing chords in the tempo of their scale, and also analyzed and applied chord structures to the scale going up and down. Follow the bass for the chords.

The Dorian (most Gregorian Chants are in Dorian) is the same rhythm up & down, what fun! The Lydian to me is {F-G} & has unique feel, sort of floating Lydian-Mixolydian back & forth (like much Reggae does). I love making positive message chants on it! ☺

One cosmic coincidence in this Synchronicity:

The rhythm of the Major Scale going up is exactly the most common Agogo or Cowbell pattern of West African sacred music. The Lydian Scale's rhythm is the 2nd most common. This is utterly mind-blowing to me and suggests there are Universal Truths and connections in our music system (called "12 makes 8") and the possession-rhythms of the African Gods!

Funny story: At a hotel in Chicago I played their pianos on all 4 floors. I was in the basement and applying Afro-Latin rhythms on Beethoven's Moonlight Sonata, really moody and weird sounding. I heard a loud crash from the kitchen and felt: oh no I made someone drop their

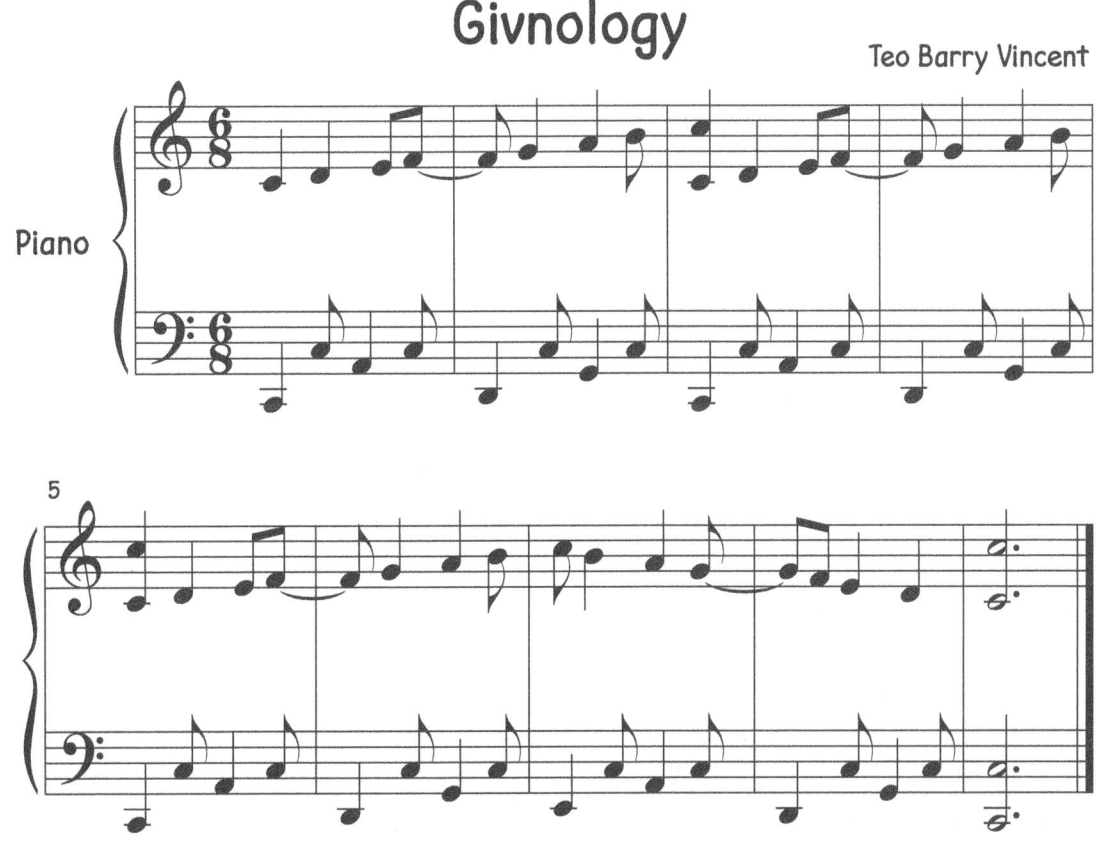

dishes! I finished my song and was leaving when I got this compliment for the first time in my life: "Bravo, brother!" I felt much better ☺.

BTW I find my favorite composers do intense music on the dominant of Db minor & I enjoy musically merging Schubert's Minuet in Db minor, List's Friska from Hungarian Rhapsody #2, Chopin's Raindrop Prelude & movements of Beethoven's Moonlight Sonata!

My 1st piano teacher Ed Bogas had me sight-reading 2 hands & jazzing it up at the same time back when I was 5 or 6 (which I haven't been able to do since, but keep working on it by sight reading). He lived next to us on Ellsworth Street in Berkeley. Later he took me & my little brother to a recording studio in SF & through a tiny window I saw Herbie Hancock & others making the weirdest music! Ed developed amazing "Studio Session" software that I marketed in Palo Alto.

Roots & Routes

A recent show about Leonardo Da Vinci posed the question: "Did he steal inventions?" At that time they called it HUMANISM where they all worked on things together. Many Master Painters had their students finish their paintings. Some Impressionists would collaborate on their paintings. Da Vinci took a draft of the parachute and improved it with specific details: wet the cloth, how to attach it to the frame, etc..

Omar Mokharti of the San Francisco School of North African Music was such a great Oud player & I would sometimes when listening note & tell him: "That is Flamenco." He would say: "No, it is ancient Berber Music; but I can't stop the Flamencos from playing it."

There is an amazing Senegalese Salsa band, their rhythm is mind-boggling. They sing amazingly but don't even speak Spanish! Japan has awesome Salsa bands too.

Roots & routes is like the bigger picture. **LINNEAGES**. Is the composer Claude Debussy from the List school (Liszt gave him some lessons) or some other teachers? Beethoven had a few teachers including Haydn and Salieri, some of his teachers he kept a secret!

There is a story where Beethoven's student Czerny said "You have to hear this young Turk!" About Czerny's student Franz Liszt. When they met Beethoven asked Liszt to play Bach's Prelude #4. Then asked List to transpose it, which he did on the spot! Beethoven kissed Liszt on the forehead and said: "You are one of the lucky ones! You will make so many people happy with your music!" Among other amazing things Liszt did is he transcribed all of Beethoven's 9 Symphonies for solo piano! How amazingly difficult!!!

Mexican Vaqueros (Cowboys) in Hawaii managed the cows, and brought the troubadour idea of traveling guitar orchestras, **Mariachis**. Eventually it ended up duos or trios with a Hula dancer. The Portuguese, the biggest immigrant group in Hawaii, brought an instrument that became the Ukulele. Most Hula songs are stuck in a time warp (not always a bad thing), many songs are in the fun style: **Swing Jazz**. Did Hawaiians have the slide guitar first, or did Country & Western musicians? Could it be an evolution from Whale Songs?

From all the Latin Music I've played for so many years, I can somehow play 3/4 Chopin songs in 4/4 Mambo Salsa! Use iTunes or Spotify to hear my Chopin Eb Prelude Nocturne in Salsa style!

J.S. Bach was made an orphan at 10 years old when his father died. He moved in with his brother who said: "Don't touch my music!" Bach proceeded to touch it, and rearranged many amazingly beautiful Vivaldi string concertos for organ performance.

In this case the beautiful musical trees of Venice, Italy, grew into German musical wisdom that was enhanced with beautiful techniques of Antonio Vivaldi (1678-1741)!

Arcangelo Corelli brought a Spanish chord sequence to Italy, **"La Folia"** or **"Follies of Spain"** which many composers rearranged such as Salieri & Handel. Handel's is now called **"Sarabande."**

Other examples of music branching out: The Jews, Blacks & Gypsies were persecuted in Spain and they got together and created **Flamenco**. Similarly the Italians, Jews & Blacks were disliked in America, they got together and created **Jazz**.

Abbe Franz Liszt's Études d'exécution transcendante d'après Paganini, S. 140, in 1838: No. 3 in A-flat minor **"La Campanella"** came from "Concerto No. 2, Opus 7" by Niccolò Paganini.

Musical Shoots took off and grew on their own!

Part II: Researches & References

Art Timeline

This was my 1st method of learning the evolution of music & other arts & sciences.

Dufay, Guillaume (1397? 1400-1474) Northern France

Artusi, Giovani Maria (1540-1613) Italian composer in 1600 stated: "They…ruin the good old rules handed down…by theorists and excellent musicians… These moderns…create a tumult of sounds, a confusion of absurdities."

Byrd, William (1539?1540?1543-1623) Lincolnshire England.
 Elizabethan period.

Vivaldi, Antonio (1678-1741) Venice Italy Composer. Most prolific and inventive of the Baroque period. Earliest music lessons from father who was in orchestra at St. Mark's cathedral. Later studied with Giovanni Legrenzi composer and leader of orchestra of St. Marks. Ordained and called "Red and priest" because of red hair. 1703 or 4 became teacher, later conductor and director at conservatory of the Ospedale DellaPieta in Venice. Conservatory also orphanage for girls. Orchestra of young girls that he wrote over 400 concertos. 40+ Operas for Venice and other cities in Italy and Germany. Last year of life moved to Vienna, didn't work out, died poor. Used clarinet. Most music remains unpublished. Goberman publisher died 1963 before completion.

Handel, George Frideric (1685-1759) Halle Germany. Wrote "The Messiah." Traveled widely. Baroque period. Father wanted him to be a lawyer. At 7 he played so well on church organ that duke of province convinced father. Studied under organist Friedrich Wilhelm Zachau. By 11 composing sonatas and church services. 1702 while student, appointed organist at Calvinist church. Hamburg joined opera orchestra as violinist. Most we know is from friend Johann Mattelson. Before 20 opera "Almira." 1707 went to Italy the home of Opera. Immersed himself in the operatic world. Instrumental duel against Domenico Scarlatti. Lost improves, organ won. Offered in 1710 job in Hanover Germany at court. November on way to London, 6 months, "Rinaldo" opera well received. Back in London 1712. Well paid. Rest of life there. April 12 1742 Messiah in Dublin Ireland first performance, instant success, but failed in England. Became success there in 1750. Had become England's favorite composer.

Bach, Johann Sebastian (1685-1750) Eisenach Germany 3/31/1685. Both parents died before he was 10. Liked French ornamental melodies and rhythms. Sang in choir. 1703 after sojourn in Weimar playing violin, organist in Lutheran church of St. Boniface in Arnstadt. 1705 left to Lubeck to hear Danish organist Buxtehude nearly 70. Congregation mad he returned 3 months late. 1707 packed harpsichord and all in hay wagon for Muhlhausen as uncle died leaving him money. Marred Maria Barbara. 1708 to Weimar became member of orchestra. Then promoted to Duke's organist. To 1717 he wrote most of his organ music. Expert in church organs – called as expert all over central Germany. Early works influenced by Reinkel and Buxtehude.. At court learned and heard Italians like Vivaldi, Corelli and Albinoni. Arranged their string concertos for solo harpsichord, ornamenting them. Concertmaster of Duke's orchestra. New compositions every month for Dukal chapel. Dukal court of Cortan employed him as conductor but got in trouble – didn't give notice. Director for Prince Leopold's orchestra. Cortan period composed bulk of secular instrumental music. After son Willlhelm Friedemann old enough to study music, wrote "teaching pieces." 20 preludes for keyboard, then others to teach son. Well-Tempered Clavier book one. Intellectual and expressive. New style combined German, French and Italian. In the midst of success, wife died in 1720 and went back to the church. 1721 married Ana Magdalena Wilcken for whom he wrote the little pieces in the notebook. 1723 – he was 38, next 25 years dedicated to the congregation of St. Nicholas church in Leipzig. Age sixty still taught and led choir.

Haydn, Franz Joseph (1732-1809) Rohrau Austria. Composer of classical – end of Baroque period. Pre-romanticism. Established "Classical." Musical construction made him "Father of the symphony and the string quartet." Viennese music made express deepest emotions. At 8 singing voice heard, joined choir in St. Stephen's church in Vienna. At 17 voice broke. Made living playing and teaching. Nicola Porpora taught him Italian and composition. Prince Anton Estrahzy heard him and made him assistant musical director. 1962 Anton died, next prince Nicholas kept him, promoted him, 30 years in employ. Wife hated music, used his music for hair curlers. Made Estrahzy's best known in Europe. Compositions played in the world at large. By 1771 composed deeper in feeling than previous. Wrote daring keys like sharp ones, introduced touches of Hungarian gypsy music. 1781 met with Mozart who admired him. Pushed Mozart more than his own. Mozart opened Haydn's ears to new delicate melodic writing. From Haydn Mozart learned the craft of putting together symphonies and quartets. Played together whenever possible. 1790 Nicolas died, next prince more into painting. 1791 went to England to cheers. 1.5 years returned with small fortune. 1794 4 new symphonies and returned to London symphony. Even King George 3rd wanted him to stay. Back in Vienna started teaching Bethovan. Requiem was by Mozart.

Mozart, Wolfgang Amadeus (1756-1791) Salzburg Austria. Pianist, violinist and conductor. Most compositions were commissioned. From simple peasant life to elegance. Father Leopold famous teacher and composer. Sister Maria Ana toured with him. Started music at 4. At 6 skilled on Organ, Harpsichord and Violin. Father took on tours Paris, London, Italy. Greeted as wonder child. Absorbed music from all countries. London wrote first symphony. 1771 returned to Salzburg to be concert-master of archbishop's orchestra. Archbishop died and next Herionymus cared less about music. 1773 discovered Haydn's string quartets. 1773-1776 wrote much. 1777 went with mother toured in Germany, France too competitive, but stayed there and composed. Paris 1778 mother died, he returned to Salsburg. 1781 finally commissioned for Opera: Idomeneo. Settled in Munich, then called back to Salsburg. Mozart and archbishop fought. Moved to Vienna – composed, performed and taught. Met Idol Haydn. Haydn helped Mozart. Played together. Emporor Joseph II commissioned "The Abduction from the Seraglio" comic romantic opera. In Vienna 1782 it was a success. Next married Constanze. Lived in gypsy fashion, gay carefree life. Dedicated 6 string quartets to Haydn. Emporor Joseph II gave consent to make "The Marriage Of Figaro." First performed in Vienna 1786. Prague Che… was Figaro-crazy! Prague Symphony (#38 in D) was success. Next wrote "Don Guivani." His greatest, "The Perfect Opera!" Later Vaugner followed idea of orchestra to underline the drama, but at that time it was too heavy for Vienna. Appointed Court Composer after Gluck's death. Paid little. Now father frenzy of composing. "A Little Night Music" "Eine Kleine Nacht Musik." "Musical Joke" full of funny forms. "The Magic Flute" written in last year, brilliant. Commissioned for "Requiem Mass" interrupting Magic Flute. Convinced Requiem was for his own death. Works listed with "K-number" for ordering in chronological order. Early works followed strict patterns of early classical period, dances, sonatas, rondos and variations are clear cut. Later forms, more personal feelings, more complex. Forms sprawl as though he were thinking out loud. Composer of Romantic period, born 50 years ahead of his time. Like 19th century composers, many colors. Concertos and sonatas did much to establish the basic style of piano writing. Long before Chopin he played with free and expressive rhythm Rubato. His piano smaller than that of today. Handling of voice never surpassed.

Beethovan, Ludwig Van (1770-1827) Bonn Germany. Master composer of symphonies, sonatas, concertos and string quartets. Father (drunkard) wanted a prodigy to make money for family. First concert at 8. 1792 sent to Vienna. Studied under Haydn. Lessons stormy because he inquired about rules. Phenomenal improvisor. After leaving Bonn no regular music work since mainly freelance composer and works for friends. Prices for various forms. Deaf he didn't give up. Conversation became difficult – people wrote down discussion. Listen to 'inner ear' for composing. In the arts stormy passion, simple directness and warm tenderness began to take the place of aristocratic elegance and grace. Music different – dramatic – from others. Soft to loud explosively. Key changes untraditional. Hammered percussive chords. Bold arpeggios. Added picallo and trombones in 5th, contrabassoon in the 9th. Clarinette replaced oboe. It was the musical form of the sonata that Bethovan changed more than anything else. Connected themes, not only 4. Foreshadowed the cyclic form of later composers. Titles made statements, music should make statements about mankind, not just idle dreams of upper classes. One of his convictions: "Man should be free!" "All mankind are brothers." His scarchzos are all musical jokes. Opera Fidelio 1805 did poorly. Life was 3 periods: youthful—first 50 opus numbers 20+ piano sonatas.. second period: greatest single step by music made by an individual composer in the history of the symphony and the history of music in general. Third period: standards people still use. Solo piano, string quartet, combination of voices and orchestra. Last works most extraordinary of all mankind. Torment brought forth some of the most sublime music. Old classical forms left far behind. Never composed quickly and easily. Many sketches in notebooks. Months even years on one theme.

Schubert, Franz (1797-1828) Vienna Austrian. The last of the classic composers, first of the romantics. Wrote classical patterns but changed to suit his own purpose and nature. Established a new form of chamber music. 600+ songs.

Mendelssohn, Felix (1809-1847) Hamburg Germany.
Brilliant composer of the early Romantic period. Family of Moses Mendelssohn philosopher. "Scottish symphony / Number 3" "Italian symphony / Number 4."

Chopin, Frederic (1810-1849) Near Warsaw Poland. "The poet of the piano." Father French mother Polish. At 20 left for Germany and never returned (heart buried in Poland, the rest in Paris). Most successful in Paris. Famous love affair with Georges Sand. Iin 1948 left for England. After a collapse returned to Paris. All piano pieces except 2 concertos focused on the piano. "Could make the piano sing" using rhythm called Rubato. In Rubato melodies are sped or slowed while tempo is constant. Must use the pedal a lot to play his music. Exploited the pianos sustaining pedal. Brought into European music dances of Hungarian music Mazurkas and Polonaise. Prelude in A Major, Opus 28 – play it!

Schumann, Robert (1810-1856) Zwikau German composer and critic. Torn between music and poetry. Mother wanted his to study law. Lost right ring finger. Untraditional styled of teaching composition. 1834 founded a newspaper for music, fighting for the highest standards of musical criticism. Edited it for 10 years under different names, "Davidsbunbler" who were ready to tear down philistines in the arts who were against new ideas. Liszt recognized his genius. He wrote about music and musicians in an informed manner. Wife Clara (daughter of Wieck his teacher whom he took to court to marry) was loved by Brahms. Eight children.

Liszt, Franz (1811-1886) Raiding Hungary. Composer, teacher and the greatest piano virtuoso. At 9 Hungarian nobleman funded studies in Vienna. Student of Czerny. Paris conservatory refused the foreigner. In Paris became friends with all the young revolutionary writers and composers who were taking part in the arts. Paganini inspired his composition style. Enormously successful. Improvised on themes given him by the audience. Support benefits for Hungarian flood victims and the statue of Bethovan in Bonn. He made Weimar the musical capital of Europe. The first to write symphonic poems for orchestra – compositions that told a story dramatically or suggested a philosophical theme. Restless experimenter in new sounds melodically and harmonically. Later music was dissonant and atonal. Whole step scale and Hungarian scales. Later lived in Rome, became A.B. Liszt.

Wagner, Richard (1813-1883) German. Excessive four-hour-long music dramas.

Foster, Stephen Collins (1826-1864) Lawrenceville near Pittsburgh Pennsylvania USA. Many of America's favorite songs. Little training. Nearby Negro churches inspired him. Father wanted businessman, at 14 wrote his first composition "Tioga Waltze" At 18 first song published. 1848 sold group including "Old Susana" to publisher for $100, became favorite of 49ers in SF. Publisher got 10,000, he decided to be publisher. Wrote many for E. P.

Christy's Minstrels. Ashamed to be known as the composer of what he called Ethiopian songs. Married 1850 but unhappy for wife and daughter – drank heavily and always in debt. When in need would sell rights to all songs for whatever he could get. "Camptown Races" and 15 other songs sold outright for $200. Wife left often. Over 200 great songs, thought of as Folk rather than composed songs. Many well known titles.

Tchaikovsky, Peter Ilyitch (1840-1893) Votkinsk (Ural mountains) Russian composer. When 10 family moved to St. Petersburg. Clerk in ministry of justice. Studied in school of Rubinstein, still working. To surprise of all he resigned to be musician. Nicholas Rubenstein hired him as professor of music theory 12 year post. His aim were compositional rather than pedagogical. Nervous collapse from overwork. Countess von Meck supported him for 13 years. Mother in law of niece. Relationship to sponser was only by correspondence. Wed unstable young woman. Tried to catch pneumonia – caught cold. Became morbid and melancholy. Madame von Meck supported him going to Switzerland, France and Italy. Wrote much gay music there. Settled down to creative life – Moscow and the country. Voracious reader. Met many bitter disappointments. Swan Lake was too symphonic. Sleeping Beauty and Nutcracker weren't well received. Piano concerto number 1 Rubenstein said unplayable, premiered in Boston in 1875. Came into demand as conductor of his own works. In 1891 was invited to conduct in NY opening of Carnagie Hall. Philadelphia, Baltimore…Returning to Russia plunged into completely different type of symphony composition.

Brahms, Johannes (1833-1897) Hamburg Germany. Late Romantic German composer. Son of all around musician. At 7 played piano. At 10 Edward Marxsen piano teacher. He became teacher. Helped family financially. Played in taverns and theatres. When at 20 Remenyi discovered him, invited to accompany. Remenyi taught Hungarian gypsy music. Remenyi introduced him to Jochim, violinist and great friend from then on. Liszt liked Brahms. Schuman proclaimed Brahms' genius in his magazine. Clara Schuman's wife made him famous playing his works at her recitals. Clara died in 1896. Life not a dramatic one. Occasional tours of Germany, Austria and Switzerland where he played and conducted. Liked long walks. 1850 his piano concertos burst upon the scene. Brought "thunder and lightning" for the piano. Brahms never wrote difficult music merely for the sake of glittering effect. 1860s wrote "Variations On A Theme By Handel" also "Variations On A Theme By Paganini." Requiem Mass successful. Later also "Variations On A Theme By Haydn." Because he showed much could still be developed, critics like Hugo Wolf and Nietze the philosopher. Never replied to attacks. Defended by Edward Hanslick, influential critic. 1881 University of Breslauv awarded honorary degree of Doctor of Philosophy, because of works had examples of his sense of humor. Instead of solemn material, several jolly German songs. After 1881 no more large instrumental groups music. 1891 turned to dark quality of clarinet. Style difficult to analyze. Unique way of saying things. Un-classical chord movements. Accused of old fashioned in his time, nowadays seen as true romantic composer who wrote poetic charged music within the old forms he loved so much.

Monet, Claude (1840-1926) French. Pioneer of Impressionist painting.

Dvorak, Antonin (1841-1904) Near Prague Czechoslovakia. Best known for Symphony in E minor "From The New World." Father butcher / innkeeper wanted him to keep family business. At 16 went to Prague. Played violin and viola in cafes and theatres to support studies. Brahms, Liszt and Smetana older folks interested and helped him get published. 1874 prize for symphony – enabling all time to composition. Home country was the old Slavic province of Bohemia, then part of Austria. Slavonic dances following Smetana following folk roots. So successful arranged for orchestra! 1876 death of oldest child, wrote "Stabat Mater." Large and small works. Touch of sweetly sad dances of homeland. 1892 to NY to become director of National Conservatory of music. Many best works written. Cello concerto beautiful. Summer in Spillvale, Iowa where there were many Czech farmers. There wrote his famous symphony "From The New World" where he tried to catch the spirit of American folk songs and spirituals. Often called #5, it was #9, arguments about whether he had really used folk melodies in it. Thrilled with the US also wrote contata to US flag, offered to write new National Anthem. A great admirer of Stephen Foster, one of the few who appreciate him. After 3 years in US homesick, returned to teach in conservatory in Prague. 7th humoresque written then. Back in Prague member Austrian House Of Lords. Symphonic poems based on the legends of Bohemia, and his opera "Rusalka" ("The Water Nymph") established him as Czechoslovakia's. most authentic musical voice. Sly little counter-melodies but never obscured clarity of music. Balanced phrases.

Edison, Thomas Alva (1847-1931) USA invented the phonograph in 1877.

Debussy, Claude (1862-1918) French. Blurred harmonies and atmospheric moods – Impressionism in music.

Sibelius, Jean (1865-1957) Finnish.
His symphonic poem Finlandia in 1900 roused patriotism and he became known as "Finland's greatest son." In Etude magazine in 1948 he stated: "Things are not good because they are old, nor bad because they are new…we must be open-minded about new experiments in music, always remembering the only standard in music is beauty."

Selected Music Styles at the Turn of the 20th Century

- **Post-Romantic**—The Romantic tradition continued with some individual changes.
- **Impressionism**—Associated most with the music of Claude Debussy, its vague and atmospheric tone paintings frequently violated traditional rules of composition.
- **Pointillism**—Written in a fragmented style, the ear is required to blend the tones.
- **Exoticism and Primitivism**—Inspired by primitive cultures and works of art, rhythm was revitalized and superseded melody in importance.

- ➤ **Neo-Classicism**—More contrapuntal textures and 18th-century forms reappeared (suites, toccatas, sonatas) using 19th–century harmonies.
- ➤ **Humor and Satire**—Some composers satirized the pretentiousness of Romantic music and poked fun at everything, including themselves.
- ➤ **Expressionism**—Intensely personal feelings were expressed with focus on dark, even weird and twisted emotions that are usually hidden from others.
- ➤ **Atonality**—Increased chromaticism and dissonance make tonal centers unclear to the listener, or the use of a tonal center or key is rejected by a composer.
- ➤ **Nationalism and Folk Influence**—Research into folk elements of various regions and countries gave greater harmonic and rhythmic variety to the musical language.
- ➤ **Cakewalk and Ragtime**—The music for the cakewalk became associated with ragtime with its "ragged," uneven, syncopated melodies over a march-like bass.

History 2   Glossary   2012 05 10

A cappella: Latin "In the chapel." Vocal only, no accompaniment. Characteristic feature of Middle Ages and Renaissance music. **Example: Haec dies**.

The "Affections:" Baroque philosophy, greco roman, state of the soul, single *affect* or clear emotion projected, "Doctrine of Affections." Vocals dramatic, depicted emotions, reaction against complex Renaissance polyphony. **Example: The Coronation of Poppea (1st performance 1642) by Claudio Monteverdi (1567-1643).**

Aria: lyrical song for solo voice accompanied by orchestra mostly. Emotional, expressing character's feelings. "**Amarilli mia bella**" by **Giulio Caccini** from 📖 **Le nuove musiche** 1602 book of monodic madrigals & arias (solos).

Arioso: short vocal passage more lyrical than a recitative but more modest in scale than an aria.

Ars nova: "new art" in Latin. Flourishing art of polyphony. Title of 14th century treatise 📖 1322 by Philippe de Vitry, 1291-1361, composer, bishop of Meaux. His motets innovated rhythmic notation: imperfect equal units not perfect 3. Historians call 14th century France Ars nova so before became Ars antiqua (old art). Isorhythm (equal rhythm) compositional technique color=melodic patterns, talea=rhythmic patterns, typically not the same length. Hocket (*French hiccup*) line split between 2 voices frequently employed.

Baroque suite: Allemande, Courante, Sarabande (optional Menuet, Gavotte, Bourré, Aria), Gigue. *French: ordre = baroque dance collections.* "Double" means a variation of the theme in French Baroque keyboard music.

Baroque: Portuguese: *barroco*, irregular pearl. Overly ornate art, 17th & early 18th centuries. **J.S. Bach.**

Bas: French: *low*, indicating volume, indoor instruments **dulcimer, lute, psaltery, rebec, recorder, vielle.**

Basso continuo: Baroque performance structure: bass as written + harpsichord or organ does *figured bass.* The whole Baroque period could be called Basso Continuo period.

Binary form: AB, 2 part, often A ends open, B closed. Common in Baroque keyboard and dance pieces.

Burgundian School: Guillaume Dufay 1397-1474, Early Renaissance. Also Giles Binchois, Antoine Busnois (Englands France): John Dunstable. France-Belgium-Netherlands, court of Dukes of Burgundy. 1st phase of Franco-Flemish School. Fauxbourdon (*French false bass*) = mid voice lowers an octave.

Cadenza: solo passage in concertos and arias, 18th century improvised. Displays soloist(s) virtuosity. Often cadential 6/4 chord proceeds it, trill on 2-3 cue back. **Mozart Piano Concerto in G Major K453.**

Canon: *Greek: law.* Polyphonic composition where each voice enters in succession with the same melody. Canons where voices enter on the same pitch are called rounds.

Camerata (florentine): Patron: **Count Giovanni de' Bardi** in Florence/*Firenze*. Wanted to recreate Greek drama. Created first operas, monodics - single voice line delivers clear expressive text (see Le Nuove Musiche 1602), oldest opera L'Euridice performed 1600. *Giulio Caccini, Jacopo Peri, Vencenzo Galilei* & patron.

Cantata: multi-movement work, recitatives, arias, ensembles& choruses. **Ein Feste Burg Ist Unser Gott**, *J. S. Bach 1715.*

Cantus firmus: "Fixed song" in Latin. Borrowed usually from Gregorian chant. Usually lowest voice. Longer melody (structural skeleton) for new polyphonic composition. Tenor = Latin *Tenere* = to hold. **Haec dies organum.**

Castrato: male soprano or alto, surgery prevents voice changing, 17th & 18th centuries, often heroic roles.

Chamber music: music for 2-10 player ensemble, 1 player per part, usually no conductor. **Trout Piano Quintet in A D667** by Franz Schubert

Chanson (*song in French*) 3 types: rondeau, virile *virelai* & ballade. Fixed forms. Secular chanson of the 14th century embraced flourishing art of polyphony, also newly secular material.

Chansonnier du Roy (Royal Songbook or Songbook of the King) anonymous late 13th century French manuscript of troubadour and trouvére songs plus 8 monophonic dances including estambie, saltarello, rondoe & basse dance. **Royal Estampie #4** Anonymous.

Chorale: hymn tune, associated with German Protentestantism, congregational therefore steps or narrow leaps, basis for many genres including cantata, often adapted Gregorian chants, SATB, **many by J. S. Bach.**

Chromaticism: Greek: *chroma* color. Includes all notes in the octave **Example: first few bars of Moro Lasso by Carlo Gesualdo** Extravagant word painting, exaggerated chromaticism with high level of dissonance, abrupt chord changes, his own texts often reflecting guilt and remorse.

Classicism: the highest level of excellence, enduring value, timeless quality. Refers to cultures of ancient Rome and Greece as well as the art, architecture and music of late 18th century. Emphasis on symmetry, balance & simplicity.

Clausulae: Roman rhetoric clausula is rhythmic figure to add finesse to a sentence or phrase. 13th century polyphonic genre with 2 strictly measured parts. A clearly defined section in discant-style organum based on a single word or syllable, often highly melismatic. *Sederunt principes* by Pérotin ca 1165-1238 is a substitute clausulae to replace Léonin's organum

Clavichord: keyboard too small for concerts. Small metal tangents strike strings. Vibrato expressive sound possible.

Clavier: *german: keyboard*, not used for organ though.

Coda: *Latin: tail=cauda*. Concluding section reaffirming the tonic key.

Concertino: the small group of instruments featured in a Baroque concerto grosso. Violin, oboe, recorder & trumpet (violone - string bass, cello & cembalo). **Brandenburg Concerto #2** by **Johann Sebastian Bach.**

Concerto: Latin: concertare = colllaborate / debate. In Italian = agree / get together. A multi-movement orchestral work, usually 3 movements fast-slow-fast. In Baroque: *solo* and *grosso*. Leading figures: Tomaso Albinoni, J. S. Bach, Arcangelo Corelli, G. F. Handel, Giuseppe Torelli & Antonio Vivaldi.

Concerto delle dona: Ferrara, Italy "Ensemble of the ladies," 3 virtuoso singers inspired composers. 16th century Renaissance madrigals repertoire. *Bell Canto started then secret knowledge?*

Concerto grosso: Baroque orchestral work usually fast-slow-fast movements, a group of solo instruments is showcased. **Brandenburg Concerto #2 by Johann Sebastian Bach.**

Consort of instruments: Renaissance term for instrumental ensemble. Whole, or broken-mixed combo.

Continuous imitation: Renaissance polyphony, theme/motive passed around voices. "Points of imitation." **Ave Maria...virgo serena**

Counter-reformation: council of Trent in Trento, Italy 1545-1563. Called by Roman Catholic Church to counter Martin Luther's reformations. **Musically: 1) the text should be audible. 2) the counterpoint should not be too dense. 3) except for the organ, instruments should not be used. 4) harmonic writing should avoid intense chromaticism. 5) use of secular *cantus firmus* banned. 6) displays of virtuosity should be avoided.** Giovanni Pierluigi da Palestrina 1525-1594 apologized for secular madrigals, "savior of polyphony." 300 motets, 100 masses including "Missa Papae Marcelli."

Counter tenor: High male strong pure tone voice. Often *falsetto*.

Cornetto: trumpet ancestor, developed from cow horn, later wood, outdoor instrument.

Crumhorn: double-reed j-shaped wind instrument. Blow into enclosed double reed. Outdoor instrument.

Dances: 16th century Renaissance: branle, pavane, galliard, saltarello, allemande. Not instrument specific. Often paired to emphasize contrast as in pavane (slow and stately) & galliard (lively and energetic). Improvisation important.

Dance suite: 17th century Baroque France *ordre* = Allemande, Courante, Sarabande, (optional Menuet, Gavotte, Bourré, Aria), Gigue. In Germany Johann Jakob Froberger standardized the order. Usually binary & same key.

Danserye 📖 Belgium dances collection 1551 by player/composer/publisher Tielman Susato ca 1515-1567.

Development: 2nd main section in sonata form. Corresponds to B of rounded binary form ABA. Exposition themes are manipulated through fragmentation, sequential treatment or changes to orchestration. Modulations and increased harmonic tension, possibly new themes. *Can be thought of as "unstable," wanting resolution.*

Discant style (of organum): original chant is faster, also called "note-against-note." Example: **Haec dies organum.**

Double: in French Baroque keyboard music this term means a variation of the theme.

Double exposition: In 1st movement of classical concertos, principal themes by orchestra establishing tonic key, then solo exposition follows where soloist supported by orchestra restates it and initiates modulation from tonic key. When soloist repeats theme(s). **Piano Concerto K453 W. A. Mozart.**

Drone: sustained pitch provides harmonic support, common in folk music.

Dulcimer: Medieval string instrument - wood soundbox, struck with hammers/mallets, indoors.

Empfindsamer: sensitive style, ppp to fff, northern Germany variety of galant style, **C. P. E. Bach.**

English Madrigal: Court of Queen Elizabeth 1st 1558-1603 had discriminating musical taste. Spread to England in the 1580s, see Musica Transalpina 1588. Different character, nonsense syllables. **Fair Phyllis by John Farmer.**

Essay on the True Art of Playing Keyboard Instruments 1753 Carl Phillipp Emanuel Bach 1714-1788

Esercizi per Gravicembalo (Exercises for Harpsichord) 500+ Keyboard sonatas by Domenico Scarlatti 1685-1757

Estampie: 13th century early Mideival dance type. Others: saltarello, ronde and basse dances. Feet stamp. **Kalenda maya by Raimbaut de Vaqueiras** & **Royal Estampie #4** Anonymous.

Exposition: 1st main section in sonata form. 2 contrasting themes are stated: 1st in tonic key, 2nd (an maybe more) are in a contrasting key, usually the dominant or relative major.

Figured bass: Baroque music shorthand: numbers below bass *realized* by *basso continuo*.

Fitzwilliam Virginal Book: early 17th century late Elizabethan / early Jacobean periods 300 keyboard works of William Byrd (Carmen's Whistle, The Ghost), John Bull (The King's Hunt), Thomas Morley & Giles Farnaby. Dances, Fantasias, preludes, arrangements of songs & madrigals & variations. Virtuosic rapid scales, ornaments & novel figures. Idiomatic approach. Named after Viscount Fitzwilliam, patron who gave it to Cambridge in 1816.

Fixed forms: rondeau, virile *virelai* & ballad*e*, 14th century *s*ecular chansons "embraced the flourishing art of polyphony." **Guillaume de Machaut 1300-1377 used fixed poetic forms ballade, rondeau & virelai.**

Fortspinnung spinning forward type of melodic writing. **Brandenburg Concerto #2 1st movement** by **J. S. Bach.**

Franco-Flemish School: Franco=French, Flemish=Flanders, includes Belgium & Holland. 15th&16th Centuries *the Dutch School, the Netherlanders.* leading figures: Johannes Ockeghem-imitative counterpoint. Josquin des Prez 1440-1521. Jacob Obrecht zangmeester at Utrecht.

Fugue: *Latin: flee.* Structured imitative contrapuntal composition where a single theme or subject prevails. **Brandenburg Concerto #2 1st movement** by **J. S. Bach.**

Fugal texture: contrapuntal composition based on imitation principle, the subject/theme pervades the entire work, entering in one voice and then another.

Genre: general term, overall character of the work and its function. Gregorian chant Haec Dies, organum Haec Dies Sederunt Principes, polytextual motet O Mitissima/Virgo/Haec Dies, monophonic chanson Ce Fut en Mai, polyphonic chanson Puis Qu'en Oubli, mass Messa de Nostre Dame Missa Papae Marcelli, dance music Royal Estampie#4 Pavane Mille Regretz, motet Ave Maria...Virgo Serena, Italian madrigal Moro Lasso al mio duolo, English madrigal Fair Phyllis, Italian opera The Coronation of Poppea, Cantata Ein Feste Burg ist unser Gott, Concerto Grosso Brandenburg Concerto#2, Orchestral Suite Water Music, harpsichord sonata Sonata in D L463/K430, Symphony #104 in D London, oratorio The Creation, opera buffa Le Nozze de Figaro, piano concerto Mozart's K453, piano sonata Pathetique in C minor op13, chamber music Trout Piano Quintet in A D667,

Goliard songs: among earliest notated secular poems. Verses in Latin, from tender love lyrics to obscene drinking songs. **Carmina Burana** *(song of Beur) 13th century. Carl Orff did in 20th century. "O, Fortuna" great song from it.*

Gradual: 4th section of Mass Proper (variable). Psalms (old testament, poetic texts) usually. Melismatic & responsoral usually. **Example: Haec dies.**

Gravicembalo: Italian for harpsichord.

Gregorian chant: Sub-form of Plainchant. Evolved from Hebrew chant tradition. Pope Gregory the great 590-604 standardized the liturgy (schola cantorum). Sacred, modal, monophonic, step or narrow leap, unmeasured rhythm. Based on sacred Latin Texts. Melodies of Roman Catholic Church Liturgical music.

Ground bass: Baroque composing device, repeated short melody under variations, often Baroque aria structure. **Example: Dido & Aeneas' "When I am laid in earth" aria - 5 measure bass pattern repeated 11 times.**

Guitarra moresca: Moorish (N Africa) origin guitar, strummed.

Harpsichord: small quills pluck strings, often 2 manuals (keyboards). Often *continuo. French: clavecin, Italian: gravicembalo.* Brandenburg Concerto #5 featured virtuoso harpsichord soloist.

Haut: French: high, volume, outdoor: cornetto (early trumpet), crumhorn, sackbut, shawm.

Heterophonic texture: simultaneous variation - variations on melody at same time. Improvisation.

Homorhythmic texture: All voices sing the same rhythm, chordal texture/homophonic, syllabic text - clear! **Fair Phyllis** by John Farmer bars 5-6 *"Feeding her flock near.." all voices sing together.*

Hornpipe: English origin dance in triple meter, associated with sailors.

Idiomatic writing Music writing that makes use of the specific properties of a particular instrument.

Improvisation In Dance Music improvisation continued to play an important role in creating music.

Indoor & outdoor instruments: haut = high (volume), bas = low volume. See those terms for instruments.

Instruments and instrumental music development in the Renaissance: Developments in music publishing contributed to greater availability and wider distribution of instrumental music. Many instruments came into being during the Renaissance: **viols from small to large, viola da gamba, virginal keyboard.**

Isorhythm: Literally equal rhythm. compositional device in **Ars nova**, combines melodic patterns (color) with rhythmic patterns (talea).

Italian Madrigal: Secular song for several voices with word painting, imitation. Most distinctive secular vocal genre of late Renaissance. Often reflective lyrics & poems. New relationship between music & poetry - generally *through-composed*. Word painting, chromatics for expressions. Venice, Ferrara (Della Dona), Mantua. Final decades of 16th & 17th centuries, mannered virtuosic style. Translated to English in: Musica Transalpina 📖 1588, 18 composer 57 piece book by editor & singer **Nicholas Yonge**. "**Moro Lasso**" by **Carlo Gesualdo.**

Keyboard Music Earliest notated music for keyboard is 1325 Robertsbridge Codex 📖. Based on vocal models and dances in Italian style. Written for instruments with range of 2 octaves. In the Baroque era keyboard instruments organ, harpsichord and clavicord became prominent instruments each with their own idiomatic repertoire.

Italian overture: orchestral genre in early 18th century. An extended work in three sections: fast-slow-fast. Formed the basis of the Classical symphony.

Le Nuove Musiche *New Music in Italian* 1602 book of monodic madrigals & arias (solos) with continuo by **Giulio Caccini 1551-1618** Florentine Camerata (di Ferenze) singer / composer. Examples & prose descriptions of monody, a new "expressive style." Vocal line ornamentation advice. Stile rappresentativo = Italian: representational style, clear text in recitative-like melody is over simple chords. Led to the development of opera.

Magnus Liber Organi Great Book of Organum late 12th centuries by **Léonin of Notre Dame School** 12th & 13th centuries **Pérotin** also (**Leoninus & Perotinus**). Léonin is the first composer of polyphony known to us by name.

Liber usualis: Latin: Book of Common Use. Late 19th century, 2000 pg chants' texts Roman Catholic services. Monophonic chants. Prepared by **monks of the Benedictine Abbey** of Solesmes, France.

Libretto: lyrics, usually based on a play, novel or episode in history.

Lute: Middle-eastern origin guitar, plucked, fretted.

Madrigal: In 14th century Italy madrigal meant poetic form and strophic (usually) musical setting as a secular song. Initially homophonic, evolved into complex polyphonic textures, more chromaticism. 16th & early 17th centuries it featured Baroque basso continuo and dramatic declamatory style. "***Moro Lasso***" **by Carlo Gesualdo.**

Major/minor tonality Sonata in D Major by **D. Scarlatti** briefly modulates to D minor.

Manheim School: Late 18th century court of Manheim, Germany group of composers: **Karl Stamitz** (standardized 4 movements not just F-S-F of French Overture), **Christian Cannabich, Franz Xaver Richter.** Developed orchestral *crescendo* and *rocket theme.* Influenced Viennese School and symphonic structure.

Martin Luther: 1483-1546 German priest. 1517 posted 95 protests on the door of Schlosskirche in Wittenberg.

Mass: prayers, readings from Bible, Ordinary = the same every week, proper = specific day's. Last Supper re-enactment called Eucharist or Holy Communion. *"Ite missa est"* (it's finished) is where the word *Mass* comes from.

Mass Ordinary: Unchanging components: Kyria **- in Greek** (&Eleison?), Gloria, Credo, Sanctus (& Benedictus?), Agnus Dei. ***Gloria from Missa Papae Marcelli by Palestrina***

Mass Proper: Variable: Intriot, Gradual, Allelua (or Tract), Offertory, Communion. ***Haec Dies= Easter Sunday***

Masses: Guillaime de Machaut 1300-1377 first polyphonic setting of Mass Ordinary with Messe de Nostre Dame (*Latin Mass of Our Lady*).

Medieval pipe: Flute ancestor, 3 holes, blown through mouthpiece.

Melismatic text setting: Many notes per syllable. Florid form, most elaborate text setting. ***Haec Dies, anonymous.***

Middle Ages: fall of Roman Empire and Constantinople (476) to the beginning of the Renaissance (1450). Instrumental Music of: not standard instruments. Church only liked organ. Oral tradition. Improvising. Processions.

Minnesinger: German: singers of love. Counterpart of French troubadours and trouvères.

Modal counterpoint: Polyphonic texture based on modes. Latin: *punctus contra punctum*, note against note.

Modes: Ancient Greek scale patterns. Tones & semitones source for Middle Ages & Renaissance musics. Referred to by their Greek names. **Ionian, Dorian, Phrygean, Lydian, Mixolydian, Aolian, Locrean.**

Modified sonata form: 18th century abbreviated sonata form, **Exposition** & **Recapitulation** but **no Development**.

Monody: *"One-song,"* late 16th century style of single vocal melody, simple accompaniment, clearer text, Florentine Camerata invented "expressive style." **Example: Amarillo Mia Bella from Le Nuove Musiche 1602 by Giulio Caccini 1551-1618** Examples & prose descriptions of monody. Madrigals & arias for solo voice & continuo. Vocal line ornamentation advice. *Stile rappresentativo = Italian: representational style*, recitative-like melody over simple chords.

Monophonic chanson: Aristocratic poet-musician *trouvères* & troubadours composed in Middle Ages, 12th &13th centuries. Songbooks 📖 called: *chansonniers.* Monophonic texture, modal melodies, usually strophic form, improvised accompaniments, texts reflected courtly love in the age of chivalry. **Ce Fun en Mai** by **Moniot d'Arras, Kalenda Maya** -oldest surviving estampie - by troubador **Raimbaut de Vaqueiras, Robin M'aime** from play by trouvéere **Adam de la Halle** -raised 4th modal melody.

Monophonic texture: Single melody line. No harmony or accompaniment. Not polyphonic. **Example: Haec dies.**

Monothematic exposition: in sonata form, theme 1 is in tonic key, then theme 2 is a transposed version of theme 1, usually up a 5th to the dominant. **Haydn's 104th Symphony.**

Motet: Sacred or secular vocal composition, rhymed, strophic, with or without instrument accomp., usually anonymous, usually contrapuntal, often polytextual in the 13th century. 15th century motet moved away from polytextuality in favor of a single text. **Ave Maria...virgo serena by Josquin des Prez 1440-1521** 4 voice a capella with cantus firmus.

Musica ficta: Latin: *false music*. Performance practice in modal music of late Medieval & Renaissance. To avoid bad intervals performers raised and lowered pitches, similar to modern-day accidentals. # or b avoided *diabolus..* **Puis qu'en oubli** by Guillame de Machaut, bar 3, Tenor and Cantus voices have a Bb, Countenor has Eb to make a perfect 5th, not tritone. Later in the same bar they need to fix: Cantus has an A and Contratenor has Eb! Tritone!

Musica enchiriadis 📖: Latin: Music Handbook. 9th century Medieval treatise for singing parallel organum. The earliest notated polyphonic music in Western art music.

Musica Transalpina 📖: Latin: Music From Beyond the Alps. 1588 18 composer 57 piece book by editor & singer Nicholas Yonge. Inspired English: Orlando Gibbons, Thomas Morley, Thomas Weelkes & John Wilbye.

Nakers: Medieval kettle drum like instrument, Middle-Eastern origin, played in pairs.

Neumatic text setting: 2 to 4 notes per syllable.

Neumes: Earliest Western art music notation. First just direction arrows. Later squares and diamonds on staff -specific pitches. **Example: Haec dies.**

Oblique organum = diaphony 1 voice: Vox organis moves away from vox principalis line. Also contrary & parallel motions.

Oboe d'amore: mezzo-soprano oboe, lower pitch, pear-shaped bell.

Oboe da caccio: alto oboe shaped like a hunting horn, pear-shaped bell, outdoor quality.

Opera: *Italian: work*. Combines vocal & instrumental music with staging and acting drama, visuals: costumes & scenery, and often dance. Created in Florence, Italy around 1600. Includes recitative, arias, ensembles & choruses. Florentine Camerata: Count Giovanni de' Bardi (patron), Giulio Caccini, Jacopo Peri, Vencenzo Galilei created Monody / Monodic style with clear melody over chords and first opera *L'Euridice*. Claudio Monteverdi elevated opera to its full artistic potential. Stile concitato, sinfonia, ground bass and opera seria are all associated with Monteverdi. Henry Purcell is the most important English Baroque composer, "British Orpheus." G. F. Handel of course brought Italian opera to England and was always well received. First public opera houses in early 17th century Italy *Oldest opera "L'Euridice" by Jocopo Perl & Giulio Caccini performed* **1600.**

Opera buffa: Italian comic opera, sung throughout, no spoken dialog, recitative secco, solos & choruses. Down-to-earth characters, fast-paced plots, farce, sexual innuendo *and political intrigues.* **The Marriage of Figaro -Mozart.**

Opera reform: Christoph Willibald Gluck 1744-1787 reformed opera in many important ways. 1) Made the overture an organic part of the score with themes from the opera. 2) Restored the chorus, long absent, making it integral to the dramatic action. 3) Reduced empty displays of virtuosity in favor of "a beautiful simplicity." 4) Minimized the contrast between recitative and aria by composing in arioso style. Operas: **Orfeo & Euridice, Alceste, Iphigenie & Tauride/Aulide.**

Opera seria: Italian: *serious opera.* Sung throughout, no spoken dialog, recitative accompagnato, solos, choruses & sinfonia musical interludes. Often historical or mythological subjects.

Oratorio: Large scale choral work, usually sacred. Word root is the place, oratory, like in a church. Traced to late 16th century. PerFor: vocal soloists, chorus and orchestra, in concert setting, no scenes, costumes or acting. One reason it flourished in Baroque Era Italy was the Roman Catholic Church's ban on opera during Lenten season before Easter. Handel adapted it to the English.

Orchestral suite: Allemande, Courante, Sarabande (optional Menuet-French origin, Gavotte, Bourré, Aria), Gigue.

Ordre: French term, means Baroque dance collections usually with many miniature dance pieces.

Organum: Earliest (9th-13th centuries) form of Polyphony - 2 or more simultaneous lines. Found in **Musica Enchiriadis** 9th century treatise. Early ones were "Parallel Organum" commonly, primary intervals, 4ths, 5ths, octaves. Léonin is the first composer of polyphony known to us by name. Clausula = clearly defined section within discant-style (original chant is faster), based on one syllable or word, highly melismatic. *substitute clausulae* composed replacing existing, as Pérotin composed new clausulae for Léonin's two-part setting of the mass. Based on Plainchant (plainsong). **Haec dies organum.**

Organ concerto invented by G. F. Handel.

Organal style: free organum, newly composed upper voices fater, "sustained-note organum" or **florid style.**

Ornamentation Carl Phillip Emanuel Bach 1714-1788 authored Essay on the True Art of Playing Keyboard instruments 1753 with instruction on all aspects including correct execution of ornaments.

Ostinato: Italian: obstinate or persistent. Rhythmic / melodic pattern repeated for an extended period.

Pairing of voices: 1st quatrain "Ave, cujus conceptio" from Ave Maria...virgo serena. "..pairing of voices, with soprano and alto followed by tenor and bass."

Parallel organum: new melodic lines added to chant. Intervals: 4, 5, 8. from: 9th century 📖 *Musica enchiriadis*

Pavane: 16th century Renaissance dance, not instrument specific. Slow in duple meter.

Piano quintet: Chamber ensemble with piano & 4 other instruments, commonly string quartet. **Schubert's "Trout."**

Plainchant: Or plain song. Judaic tradition. Monophonic texture, modal melody, narrow melodic range, flexible and unmeasured "prose" type of rhythm.

Polyphonic texture: Independant melody lines / voices simultaneously. referred to as "contrapuntal" texture. **Fair Phyllis** by **John Farmer.**

Polyphonic chanson: Secular chanson of the 14th century Ars Nova 📖 1322 by Philippe de Vitry 1291-1361, composer, bishop of Meaux, newly secular material **Puis qu'en oubli** by **Guillaume de Machaut.**

Polyphony: end of Romanesque period (c. 850-1150) with more precise notation music progressed from improvisation to carefully written, during Gothic era (c. 1150-1450) rise in cathedrals, choirs, organs, *composer is Latin: componere*, to put together. Léonin is the first composer of polyphony known to us by name.

Pollytextual motet:: Simultaneous texts, usually 3 voices, bottom is cantus firmus. Primary intervals (4 5 8). Upper voice more active. 13th Century. **De ma dame vient/Diex, comment porrie/Omnes** by Adam de la Halle trouvére / **O mitissima/Virgo/Haec dies.**

Portative organ: Medieval portable keyboard, high-pitched pipes, bellows pumped "organetto".

Positive organ: Larger 14th century portable organ, one keyboard, no pedals, small pipes.

Psaltery: Medieval *dulcimer like* string instrument - trapezoidal wood soundbox, fingers or plectrum, indoors.

Prose rhythm: no bar lines or note values indicated, text flows naturally.

Quatrains means verses, duplet = 2, quatrain = 4

Rebec: violin like Medieval indoor 3 string pear shaped bowed string instrument, played on the arm or under chin.

Recitative: speech-like singing, declamatory. More dialog than lyrical aria. Sometimes replaced by regular speech. Used in operas, oratorias and cantatas.

Recitative secco: Italian: *dry recitative*. Speech-like, declamatory singing style, only supported by *continuo*. Used in opera, oratoria and cantata. **"Thy hand, Belinda" from Dido and Aeneas** by **Henry Purcell**

Recitativo accompagnato: Italian: *accompanied recitative*. Speech-like but supported with ensemble/orchestra. Allows for greater connection with the text. Stronger emotion portrayed. More likely in strict time.

Recorder: Medieval into Baroque end-blown indoor instrument.

Reformation: MLuther 1483-1546 1517 posted 95 theses. Translation to people's language. Henry VII 1509-1547 separated from Rome, formed Anglican Church 1534. Council of Trent in Trento, Italy 1545-1563 reaffirmed Catholicism - Counter-Reformation: cantus firmus banned. Giovanni Pierluigi da Palestrina 1525-1594 "Perfect reflection of the ideals of the Council of Trent and Counter Reformation." "Saviour of polyphony."

Regal: 14th C smaller organ, reeds, strap around neck, like harmonica, bellows pumped.

Renaissance motet: sacred or secular a capella rhymed strophic poem usually contrapuntal. 15th century motet moved away from polytextuality in favor of a single text. **Ave Maria...virgo serena by Josquin des Prez 1440-1521** *4 voice a capella with cantus firmus.*

Responsorial singing: Renaissance and Middle Ages method of performance, "Verse" solo alternates with "Responce" choral passages. **Haec dies.**

Rhythmic modes: 1) long-short, 2) s-l, 3) l-s-s, 4) s-s-l, 5) l-l, 6) s-s-s.

Ripieno: *Italian: full / complete.* Also called *tutti*. Means the full orchestra in Baroque concertos.

Ritornello: tutti / ripieno alternation with ritornello is the returning of the main theme / episode / solo or concertino. Recurring theme functioning as a refrain in Baroque compositions, can be intro or postlude in arias or choruses or a unifying thread in a concerto. **Cantata #80 "Ein feste Burg ist unser Gott"** by Bach opens with a festive ritornello.

Ritornello form: In the 1st and/or 3rd movements of Baroque concertos often the opening passage (ritornello) is restated throughout the movements. **Brandenburg Concerto #2 1st movement by J. S. Bach.**

Ronde: Renaissance round dance outdoors in a circle or line.

Rondeau: Popular fixed poetic form of polyphonic chansons of **Ars Nova**, 4 verse + refrain, AB aA ab AB.

Rondo form: ABACA or ABACABA or similar. A is at least 3 times in tonic key. B & C contrast the key and thematic material. **"Pathetique" Piano Sonata Op. 13 2nd Movement.**

Rounded binary: 2 part form, A - BA, some of A returns within B. **Sonata in D Major by D. Scarlatti.**

Sackbut: French: pull-push, trombone ancestor, outdoor.

Sacred music development in the Renaissance: Role played by Josquin des Prez significant Franco-Flemish School composer. Pursued his profession in Italy, working for powerful Sforza and d'Este families, also churches including the Sistine Chapel in Rome. Giovanni Pierluigi da Palestrina Devotion to the Church was so strong he formally apologized for writing secular madrigals in his youth.. 5 movements of the Ordinary, **Missa Papae Marcelli** and it's great clarity in text setting, well-balanced polyphonic texture earned him "savior of polyphony" title.

Secular vocal music in the Renaissance: "..in the 16th and early 17th centuries, 'madrigal' denoted a type of secular song that flourished in the small aristocratic courts of Italy, including Venice, Ferrara, and Mantua; it then gained widespread popularity in Europe and England." **"Moro Lasso" by Carlo Gesualdo.**

Shawm: Middle Eastern origin oboe ancestor, shrill nasal tone, double reed, outdoor.

Singspiel: German comic opera, includes spoken dialogue. **The Magic Flute by W. A. Mozart.**

Sinfonia: Baroque generic term, Monteverdi meant an instrumental movement. Transition scenes in operas. **The Coronation of Poppea, Act 3, Scene 7 by Claudio Monteverdi.**

Sonata cycle: Multimovement structure emerged in the Classical era in symphony, sonata and concerto.

Sonata form: "First movement form," "Sonata-allegro form," is usually the 1st movement of a sonata cycle, **Exposition**=statement of 2+ themes often contrasting, **Development**=departure & **Recapitulation**=return. Like binary 1st half moves from tonic to dominant, 2nd half back (sonata form often called compound binary), like ternary (ABA) form - exposition - development (contrast) - recapitulation. With B section of rounded binary development in other than dominant key, sonata form came into existence. J. G. Harrer 1703-1755, Bach's successor at Leipzig, advocate of Galant style, and other composers in the 1730s in incipient sonata form, B sections manipulating thematic material but without development sections, also found in D. Scarlatti and C. P. E. Bach's. Transition from binary and rounded binary to sonata-allegro form was crafted greatly by **Domenico Scarlatti's 500 Keyboard Sonatas**.

Sonata form functions: *"Outline the main sections of Sonata form and explain how they function. make reference to two or more specific works to illustrate your points."* **Sonata in D, L 463 / K 430 by D. Scarlatti**: *4 bar phrase repeated creates symmetry. Harmonic structure I IV V chords. Tasteful trills. B section modulates to the dominant key, A major. Romantic dissonance with D minor figure over dominant pedal. End of B section coda is back in the tonic key. Foreshadows sonata form.* **London Symphony #104 in D by F. Haydn**: *Exposition melody symmetrical. Second theme modulates up a 5th (double exposition, same theme transposed). Development goes into B minor and other keys. Recapitulation back into D Major.* **"Cosa Sento!" from The Marriage of Figaro by W. Mozart**: *the Count sings theme 1 in Bb, theme 2 by Susanna is up a 5th, "Sonata form perfectly matches the action, the recapitulation fraught with irony..."*

Stile concitato: Italian: *agitated style*. Monteverdi's term, expresses *hidden tremors of the soul*. Use of *tremelo* & *pizzicato* instrumental ornamentation and rapid repeated vocal notes. vocal tremelo on "Imperial" **Coronation of Poppea Scene 7, Coronation.**

Stile rappresentativo: Italian: *representational style*. Florentine *Camerata* musicians described their monodic style, recitative-like melody over simple chords. **Example: "Amarilli mia bella" by Giulio Caccini.**

String quartet: most popular Classical era chamber ensemble. 2 violins, viola and cello. Genre refers to compositions written for this same ensemble. 4 movements usually, **fast-slow-medium-fast**.

Strophic form: Same music for every verse, not *through-composed*, less connection between words & music. **Ce Fun en Mai by Moniot d'Arras.**

Sturm und Drang (Storm and stress): movement in German literature c. 1760-85 with the artist's aim of frightening, shocking, stunning, overcoming with emotion. In music: passionate outbursts, dark stormy moods, Haydn's minor key sonatas 1770 #44, #49 and C. P. E. Bach's Prussian sonatas and symphonies. In opera: Gluck's scene with the furies in Orfeo et Euridice, the conclusion of Mozart's Don Giovanni.

Suite: usually same key, usually different dances.

Syllabic text setting: one note per syllable, text heard clearly.

Symphony: In early 18th century string orchestra with continuo was the standard ensemble. Handel & Bach explored wind instruments. Now 4 families (consorts) strings, woodwinds, brass & percussion. Italian overture's 3 sections fast-slow-fast was an origin. Manheim School developed orchestral crescendo & rocket theme, members: **Christian Cannabich, Franz Xaver Richter** composer **Karl Stamitz** (standardized 4 movements not just F-S-F of French Overture), inserted (the ternary) menuet & trio making the 4 movement sonata cycle sonata form. Also evolved from binary and rounded binary structures as in many Scarlatti keyboard sonatas..

Tabor: Medieval large cylindrical drum percussion.

Tattle: tenor oboe, pear-shaped bell.

Tambourine: wooden frame with small metal disks striked or shaken.

Tenor: Tenere = Latin, to hold. In Mid Ages polyphonic composition the Cantus Firmus borrowed material.

Terzetto: Italian term for "trio." Musical number for 3 voices / characters.

Ternary form: 3 part form, ABA, B often creates contrast, used often in Baroque arias.

Terraced dynamics: Baroque style of stark contrast by changing dynamics abruptly.

Texture: Polyphic often imitative, homorhythmic, monody, monophonic.

Theme and variations: Often a slow movement of a sonata cycle. Theme melody statement, then transformations / variations to melody, harmony, rhythm or orchestration. *Franz Schubert 's* **Trout Piano Quintet 4th movement**

Treatise on the Fundamentals of Violin Playing 1756 Johann Georg Leopold Mozart 1719-1787

Tremolo: rapid alternation between 2 notes or notes of a chord. **"Pathetique" Piano Sonata Op. 13 Exposition.**

Troubadour: word means "finder" or "inventor." Aristocratic poet-musician, composer in S. France. Monophonic chansons such as **"Kalenda Maya" by Raimbaut de Vaqueiras**. Monophonic texture, modal melodies, usually strophic form, improvised accompaniments, texts reflected courtly love in the age of chivalry.

Trouser role: Male character performed by a soprano, mezzo soprano or contralto. Roles first created for male *castrati* frequently turned into trouser roles for modern performances. **Cherubino in Marriage of Figaro**.

Trouvère: finder or inventor. Aristocratic poet-musician, composer in N. France. **"Ce fut en mai" by Moniot d'Arras** monk, last in a long line of trouvéres, ca 1213-1239. Monophonic chansons, solo singer. strophic, langue d'oil. Also: *trouvéere* **Adam de la Halle.**

Vielle: Medieval violin ancestor. Figure 8 shape, played with a bow, indoors.

Viennese School: as capital of Austria, it was a leading dynamic progressive cosmopolitan center in the late 18th century, the "Age of Enlightenment" when knowledge, rational thinking and equality was replacing opulent, ornate Baroque era, more Greco-Roman (architectural) clean lines, simplicity, proportion, balance, symmetry: *Classical Ideals. Vien* is at the crossroads between Europe & the East, attracted leading artists, architects, musicians and writers. The Classical era masters, all associated with Vienna are **Haydn, Mozart, Schubert** & **Beethoven**.

Virtuosic writing: Fitzwilliam Virginal Book style of writing often virtuosic. Also: Henry Purcell 1659-1695 was a prolific composer with virtuosic keyboard style. **His suites**.

Viol: viols = Renaissance bowed instrument family.

Viola da gamba: 6 strings, between legs (gamba means leg) like cello, fretted like a guitar.

Virginal: in Renaissance Era England, term for plucked keyboards. Smaller than harpsichord, simpler. Italian / Flemish different shapes, English always rectangular.

Word painting: Musical pictorialization. Music reflects text meanings. **Madrigals, operas and oratorios**.

Brown text we were not told to put in glossary but I wanted to. Review reflections in green. Examples are in bold italic.

Great Composers

Vivaldi, Antonio (**1678 Venice Italy** –1741 Vienna Austria). Red Priest, Father of the Concerto

Earliest music lessons from father who was in orchestra at St. Mark's cathedral. Traveled widely. Later studied with Giovanni Legrenzi composer and leader of orchestra of St. Marks.

- 1703 ordained. 3 or 4 became teacher, later conductor and director at conservatory of the Ospedale DellaPieta in Venice. Conservatory also orphanage for girls. Orchestra of young girls.
- 1711-29 Published in Amsterdam (Etienne Roger) larger plates. 1725 Opus 8 "Competition between Math & Inspiration"-4 Seasons!
- 1737 Opera shut down by Pope!

Wrote over 500 concertos, 230 for solo violin. 40+ Operas for Venice and other cities in Italy and Germany. Last year of life moved to Vienna-had connection to Emperor, didn't work out, died poor. Used clarinet. Most music remains unpublished. Goberman publisher died 1963 before completion.

Handel, George Frideric (1685 Halle Germany -1759).

Wrote "The Messiah." Traveled widely. Baroque period. Father (surgeon to Saxon duke) wanted him to be a lawyer. At 7 he played so well on church organ that duke of province convinced father. Studied under organist Friedrich Wilhelm Zachau. By 11 composing sonatas and church services. When 12, dad, 70, died.

- 1702 while student, appointed organist at Calvinist church. Hamburg joined opera orchestra as violinist. Most we know is from friend Johann Mattelson. Before 20 opera "Almira."
- 1703 to Hamburg "free city," met Teleman, they traveled to Lube to meet Buxtehude (80!).
- 1705 first opera Almira a success! Dueled, survived, 1706 inheritance – took "Grand Tour," stayed years in Italy.
- 1707 went to Italy the home of Opera. Immersed himself in the operatic world. Instrumental duel against Domenico Scarlatti. Lost improves, organ won. Offered in 1710 job in Hanover Germany at court. November on way to London, 6 months, "Rinaldo" opera well received (1707?).

Oratorio, cantatas, He & Scarlatti had Harpsichord competition!

- 1709 Venice "Agrippina" Nero's Rome.
- 1710 appointed Kappelmeister (Chapel Master) by Prince George Louis – elector of Hanover.
- 1711 London, Queen Ann, Rinaldo successful, 1712 back she commissioned works 1714 died, prince became King George I, boss!
- 1719 Royal Academy of Music to produce Italian Opera. Opera Seria 1924-5 "Julius Caesar in Egypt," "Tamerlane," "Rodelinda." Strong character god divas Bordoni & Cuzzoni to agree! ☺☺
- 1702
- April 12 1742 Messiah in Dublin Ireland first performance, instant success, but failed in England. Became success there in 1750. Had become England's favorite composer.

Bach, Johann Sebastian (1685 Eisenach Germany –1750).

Left orphanage at 10 and brother Johan Christoph raised him.. Liked French ornamental melodies and rhythms. Sang in choir.

- 1703-7 Arnstadt Organist in Lutheran church of St. Boniface. 1705 trip to Lubeck to hear Danish organist Buxtehude nearly 70. Congregation mad he returned 3 months late.
- 1707 packed harpsichord and all in hay wagon for Muhlhausen as uncle died leaving him money. Marred Maria Barbara.
- 1708 to Weimar became member of orchestra. Then promoted to Duke's organist & chamber musician through to 1717 he wrote most of his organ music. Expert in church organs – called as expert all over central Germany. Early works influenced by Reinkel and Buxtehude.. At court learned and heard Italians like Vivaldi, Corelli and Albinoni. Arranged their string concertos for solo harpsichord, ornamenting them.
- 1717 Concertmaster of Duke's orchestra. New compositions every month for Dukal chapel, Dukal court of Cothen employed him as conductor but got in trouble – didn't give notice. Director for Prince Leopold's orchestra. Cothen period composed bulk of secular instrumental music. After son Willlhelm Friedemann old enough to study music, wrote "teaching pieces." 20 preludes for keyboard, then others to teach son. Well-Tempered Clavier book one. Intellectual and expressive. New style combined German, French and Italian. In the midst of success, wife died in 1720 and went back to the church.
- 1721 married Ana Magdalena Wilcke for whom he wrote the little pieces in the notebook. 1722 & 1742 **Das Wohltemperirte Clavier.**
- 1723 – he was 38 Leipzig St. Nicholas church for next 27 years. 1729 Appointed director **Collegium Musicum**.

1747 Visited son Carl Phillip Emanuel working for Frederick the Great in Potsdam. King suggested theme, Bach improvised a great fugue. Later composed & sent **Musical Offering** to great monarch. Passions: St. John 1724, St. Matthew 1727. Christmas Oratorio 1734, Mass in B minor 1749. 6 English & 6 French suites, etc., etc. Art of Fugue unfinished. 200+ cantatas, 150+ choral preludes. Concertos for up to 4 harpsichords!

Haydn, Franz Joseph **(1732 Rohrau Austria** -1809). "Father of the symphony and the string quartet."

Established "Classical." At 8 singing voice heard, joined choir in St. Stephen's church in Vienna. At 17 voice broke. Made living playing and teaching. Nicola Porpora taught him Italian and composition. Prince Anton Estrahzy heard him and made him assistant musical director in Esterhaza.

1762 Anton died, next prince Nicholas kept him, promoted him, 30 years in employ. Wife hated music, used his music for hair curlers. Made Estrahzy's best known in Europe. Compositions played in the world at large. By 1771 composed deeper in feeling than previous. Wrote daring keys like sharp ones, introduced touches of Hungarian gypsy music.

1781 met with Mozart who admired him. Pushed Mozart more than his own. Mozart opened Haydn's ears to new delicate melodic writing. From Haydn Mozart learned the craft of putting together symphonies and quartets. Played together whenever possible.

1790 Nicolas died, next prince more into painting. 1791 went to England to cheers, composed 12, Symphony #94 performed 1792, **"Surprise"**, in G Major – sudden fortissimo crashing chord in the slow movement to wake up the audience! 1.5 years returned with small fortune. 1794 4 new symphonies and returned to London symphony. Even King George 3rd wanted him to stay. Back in Vienna started teaching Beethovan.

1798 Die Schopfung (The Creation). 1801 Die Jahreszeiten (The Seasons). Both Sacred vocal music. 14 operas. 40 sonatas. Requiem was by Mozart.

Musicionary

Baroque Suite: Allemande, courante, sarabande & gigue. Optional: minuet, gavotte, bourrée, passepied, hornpipe. Sometimes has an overture.

Binary form: AABB (~ternary ABA). Rounded binary brings back a theme later.

Col legno: play violin with wood of bow. Example: Symph. Fantastique – last dance tune alternating with loud brass statements of Dies Irae.

Cantus firmus: fixed melody, a longer melody embellished by voices' elaborate ornamentation.

Concerto: orchestral, 2violins, violas, cellos, wood etc.. with contrasting dynamics, usually 3 movements Fast-Slow-Fast

Concerto grosso: opposition between small group concertino and large tutti or ripieno group. Arcangelo Corelli was early contributor.

Da capo aria: Lyrics in ternary ABA form in operas, cantatas & oratorios.

Embellishments: melodic decorations.

French Overture: Slow (often repeated) - **Fast** (~FSF of Italian Overture)

Genre: type of music (Opera, Concerto, Sonata

Ground bass: repeated low voice phrase, upper voices independent of it.

Hemiola: grouping1/4 in 2 suggesting 2/4 or 3/2

Homophany: one voice is prominent over accompanying lines or voices.

Homorhythmic: voices on the same rhythm.

Hetrophony: multiple voices on same melody together. ~Monophony

Kyrie: first part of mass.

Mambo: syncopated quadruple (4) meter Afro-Cuban dance rhythm.

Mass: 1) Kyrie, 2) Gloria, 3) Credo, 4) Sanctus, 5) Agnus Dei.

Minuet & Trio: never sonata form, always compound ternary form.

Modulation: change tonal center, usually to dominant (V).

Monody: make words clearer, one melody accompanied using rhythms of speech.

Monophony: single voice alone.

Motive: motif, small fragment of a theme.

Movement: complete, comparatively independent division of a large-scale work.

Sequence: Idea restated at a higher or lower pitch.

Solo concerto: for solo instrument and accompanying group (~concerto grosso) usually Allegro-Adagio-Allegro

Sonata-allegro form: sonata form, first-movement form,
1) themes stated in the **exposition** •
2) developed in the **development** •
3) restated in the **recapitulation**.

Sonnet: Poem 14 lines long.

Strophic form: repeated music for each stanza of text.

Oratorio: large scale dramatic genre based on religious serious text. Opera with no costumes or scenes or action.

Ostinato: Ground Bass, a repeated idea.

Polyphonic: 2 or more melodic lines combined into multivoiced texture. ~ Monophonic. "*Polyphony* describes a many-voiced texture based on *counterpoint* -one line set against another.-p23"

Polyrhythm: Several rhythmic patterns or meters, common in 20th century music and certain African musics.

Polytonality: Simultaneous use of two or more keys, common in 20th century music.

Program Music: Program Symphony, Word Painting, the music portrays words.

Recapitulation: restatement of exposition, third movement of Sonata-allegro form, usually in tonic.

Recitative: solo vocal declamation that follows the inflections of the text, often disjunct style. Found in opera, cantata and oratorio. Secco or accompagnato.

Ritornello: short passage unifies the work by recurring again later.

Rocket theme: quickly ascending rhythmic melody used in Classical-era instrumentals. Credited to composers in Mannheim, Germany.

Rondo: ABABA, ABACA & ABACABA returning in the tonic. In multimovement forms, the last movement.

Sacred cantatas: multimovement works with solo arias, recitatives & choruses, with orchestral accompaniment.

Scherzo: ABA usually triple meter. Haydn helped Scherzo-Trio replace Menuet-Trio in Sonata-allegro form compositions.

Serenade: genre combines chamber music and symphony. Related to divertimento and cassation.

Symphonic Poem: Tone Poem. One-movement orchestral form develops poetic idea suggesting scene, mood.

Tempos: presto=very fast, vivace=lively, allegro=fast, moderato=moderate, andante=walking page, adagio=quite slow, largo=very slow, grave=slowest. Accelerando=speed up, ritardando=slowing down (same as ritenuto on scores). Allegro con brio=with vigor.

Ternary: ABA, statement-departure-restatement. "Ternary form, with its logical symmetry and its balance of the outer sections against the contrasting middle one, constitutes a clear-cut formation that is favored by architects and painters as well as musicians.-p28"
Verismo: realism in opera. 1890s Italy brought naturalism to lyric theatre.
Vocables: syllables without meaning.
Word painting: rich musical pictorialization of imagery. Program music? Tone Poems are.

Non-Chord-Notes

Circle a non-chord note and specify using LABEL:

Non-chord Note	Label	Approach	Departure	Metrical Position
Passing note	pn	by step	by step, same direction	weak
Accented pn (**app**-SS)	apn	by step	by step, same direction	strong
Neighbor note (**un/ln**-SS)	nn	by step	returns to previous pitch	weak
Accented nn (**app**-SS)	ann	by step	returns to previous pitch	strong
Incomplete nn (**un/ln**-SS)	inn	by leap	by step	weak
Appoggiatura	app	free	by step	strong
Échappé	éch	by step	by a 3rd, with a change of direction	weak
Suspension	susp	prepared	by step, usually downward	strong
Cambiata (**un&ln**-syllbs)	camb	by step	**un** then **ln** then returns	both weak
Anticipation	ant	free	holds the pitch	weak

Ice-Cream-Chords

SetLists (sharing helpful "Musical Shorthand")

Talking Beat Sets (p1)

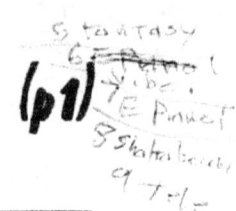

A 1 — Double Trouble

Percussion words - Hit, words - Hit, Hit with words, Hi Hit, Hi Hit, buildup, Jam, 8 hits, Jam, at same place out

A2 (+Encore) — Ola Oluwa — A Major

King Soni Ade, Synth(21), Glocken(16)
(21-oct down) {a a a b b c# c# d {c# b c# d c# d e e f#} d d d c# c# b b a} (16) {A A A ® e f# e A A a e f# e f# -- fit in A A7 D B-} "I am for Joy..." A A B- A, hits: {A, G G A A A}, cued to (21) top out

A 3 — Morisisikan — D Major

Old Highlife, Celeste(17)
(17) Guitar line, {d a a f# a ® f# a ® a e a a g a ® g a ®} Guitar line to D! hit break, back, D D D D break, perc solo, ____ ?

A 4 — Ashe — A minor

King Soni Ade, Synth(21), Epiano(14)
(21) Guitar, c g a a g a ® c b c b a g a ® c g a a g a ® c d e g a g a a (14) A- A- A- A- A- G A- ! {® g a c a g a g a}∞ A- A- A- A- A- G A- ! {a a c c d d e ® e g d e c d a ® c d a c b c g e a a} e a a ® e a a [perc solo] cued to groove cued to A- A- A- A- A- G A- !

B 1 — Esubiribiri — E Major

Celeste(17)
(17) {E ® b c# F#- ® c# b c#} 4 E Hits, {e ® g# b e d# c# b d# ® f# a d# ® c#} = E to B faster montuno.

B 2 — Olomi Jowo — E Major

Celeste(17)
(17) {E E A (B)}

B3 (+Encore) — 365 — A Major

Celeste(17), Alarm(PD9), MetalKeys(21)
(17) ® A A ® A A ® E E ® E E ® A A ® with guitar's last note A∆ {® A A ® A A ® B B B ® B B ® E7 E7 E7 ® E7 E7 ® A A ® A A fit in with 2nd "...my number" A E7 A} top again, groove again, their line hold e+5th, ( ) A- chord LYNS solo, line: e g d e c c a a a c c c a a e e, chord over SOJI solo - WITH 5 Am HITS, line, no chord DOMINICO / perc solo, phone (D9), ( ) line, (17) 1 melody, ( ) line!

B 4 — Lady — Eb Minor

Fela Juju, EPiano(14)
(14) {Db Eb- Eb- (4 and 1) ®}4x low eb {® f eb ® db eb eb}4x , Eb- Jam - end with beginning, then retard "4 - and - 1"

Arboribus Musicorum *Trees of Music* • Part 2 • Page 30

Repertório do Ivson 531-4630   HSP=Horns, Strings, Piano Compiled Friday, September 3, 1993

1. **Toque De Fole\C\Samba\Accordian**

    CHART√ {g-c-b-bb-®-f-g-a-B-F-C}4x C9-F6/9 "A"={C-Bb-C-Bb-F-G-C-(C9-F6/9)1st3x} "B"={Bb-C}4x "A" "B" "A" E7-{Am-E7-Am-Am-Bb-F-G-C} "A" dc

2. **Pelo Amor De Deus\EbΔ\Djavan/HSP**

    CHART√ D4-3-2-1} "A"={1-6-2-5-1-7-b7-3-2-b6-5} 2-5-3-6-7-3-6

3. **Decote Pronunciado\FΔ\Morais Moreira/HSP**

    CHART Bb line, "A"={1-2-3-1-2-3-6-2-2(-5-b2-1)1st x} "B"={4-2(7)-1-6(7)-2-5} dc, line, {2-5-1-6}∞

4. **O Menino\FΔ\Samba/HSP**

    CHART 1-1-2-5-3-6-2-5-1 "A"={3-2-5-1-f-e-d-c-®-1-6(7)-2-5-1-6(7)-2-5-1-6-2-5-3-6-2-5-1-6-2-5-1} {2-2-1-2-2-5-1} "A"1x

5. **Take Me\GΔ\Djavan/HSP**

    Chart in Ab {2-3-2-3-4-5 "A"={1-2}4x { 1 - 2 }6x { 6 - 4(7) - 2 - 4(7) }4x -4 "A"2x -4(7)∞ "Intro tatakata"

6. **Bird of Paradise\EbΔ\Djavan/HSP**

    Chart in F corrected { 1 - 6 - 5 - 4 - 5 }

7. **Apple\Eb-\Djavan/HSP**

    CHART {f-bb-c-f}Circular(C# bass) {Bm-®-F#7-F-

8. **Real\Bb-\Djavan/HSP**

    Chart in F { ® - f - eb - db - bb - ® - f - d - bb } Eb- - B - Bb - A - Ab - db - f# - F- - Bb7 - Eb- - B - Bb - A - Ab - Db - Bb - Eb__ {B- - B - B- - B - Bb- - Bb- - BΔ - B- BΔ - B- - Bb- - ® - Bbø - Eb7(-9)

1. **Isso Aqui (medly)\ \ /**

    CHART in? Stgs: d#-g#-d#-c#-b-g-d#-c#-g#/b-f#/b hold : c#-d-d#-e -b-c-®-b-c#-d 2ndx: g#-a-b-c-e-b-b-c#-g#-f#

2. **Bom Dia, Boa Tarde\Bb-\ /StringsPiano**

    Chart in B-

3. **Ta - Mahal (medly) Rio Para Grassie\F#-\ /**

    Booklet"A"={ 4- - 5- - 1- }∞ // E- "B"={ 1-6-7 } G "C"={1-3-4-5}4x 6-5-4-5-1-1 "C" {C7 - G-} C7 - D7 "C" wail G

4. **Rolinha\EΔ?\ /SalsaPiano ±Horn**

    Chart in G changed to E {1-6-2-6-2-6-1} {1-1-1-2-5-5-1-1-6-6-2-2-5-5-5-5-1-1-6-6-2-2-5-5-1-1}

5. **Dois Neguinhos\F#Δ\ /H, Strings**

    CHART {C# - B - F#}3x B - C# - F# "A"={1 - 1 - 5 - 5 - 2 - 5 - 1 - 1} {5 - 5 - 1 - 1}7x {5

6. **Toda Forma De Amor\A-\ /**

    Booklet "A"={A- - G}∞ "B"={G - A}

1. **I Shot The Sherrif\F-\Reggae\Organ**

    line {1-1-4-5} {4-5-1-1} 2-5-1 line 'extended bass line, guitar solo, head, out.

2. **Leve Senseção**

3. **Ela**

4. **Is This Love**

5. **Beez M\G-**

6. **Fung Uh Nung**

7. **Beez Melody\C**

8. **I Just Called\C**

1. **Ashe Ashe**
2. **..**
3. **Dance\B-**
4. **Maracangalha\F#**
5. **Bundalele\EΔ**

    4-1

6. **Odé Adão**
7. **Cheiro De Suar\C#-\Reggae/Organ**
8. **Embala Trilegal\A-\ /Strings**
9. **Namorad Da Chuva\C#**
10.   **OLODUM**
1. **Ven Morena\A\6/8 AfroPeru/**
2. **Rastafari\F-\Reggae/**

    {1-1-4-5}

4. **Rio Paragussú\F\Lambada/**

5. **A Cura\D\ /**

    Booklet

Barnstormin (Ball Game) • EM (A Capella)
Mbaqanga • Reggae • C F Gsus ^G • Piano DXFlute

In/Out=C ® Em ® F ® Am ^G FG C! ® Em ® F ® D-C-B D C! ®. flute w CH&horns
{(2)e g e a   a c e-c-d (b 2ndX)} 4thCh®

Ootsotsi • Am4 G4 • Bubble/Bang - Siren/Synth choir#83

(I?) Intro=Siren + Pad Am9 long time, in∞, Dub, long ® riddim

One World • Cm Bb Ab Bb • Bang Bong/Pad Strings intro

Intro= {Cm4 Bb4 Ab4 Bb4}2x, {Cm2 Bb2 Ab2 Bb2}4X-break, verse&chs=4s
CHline=(1and){g bb g bb c g f} ®), guitarsolo=2s, back for verse, end=bb bb! c c   bb! c c

Qinebe • Am4 Dm4 • Funky! • (MANUAL)Bang DXClav&Synth solo

In=drums. Dumile rap Bass change. no bass w CH. 2nd rap:solo

Natty Dread • Am2 G2 • Bubble/Bang/Effects#84(MANUAL)

Guitar starts. intro={Gm4 Dm4}4x pad, chorus={Am2 G2}, verse={F2 G2 Am3 G1 F2 G2 Am4}3x, back, Guitarsolo=chorus&verse(2X), 2X, dub, riddim

Going Around • D2 G2 A4 • Highlife • Rain/Trans Organ/Marimba

(I) Long drone intro,{6 ch ®}, ..3123 " " .. part _____

Makube Njalo/War • A4 D2 Bm2 E4 A2 E2 • High Organ#34

(I) Intro=slow{D A D A Bm A E A}, Aswers. ends: e-e d c# b a

Sidudla • F F Gm C • Soft Accordian #40

(I) 1-and etc..., pieces drop out for end - to Perc. solo

Guluva • G G C D • Soft Organ

(I) after 2 claves. break=d ® d! d! d-c-b-a- ,ends d-c-b

D.V.'s Gospel • Gm4 Cm2 Dm2 Gm3 Dm-Dm • Organ/DXClav

guitar starts, horns, I'm in wit bass {Gm, pad 4&5, Gm^Gm Dm-"}, bubble verse 2x, same w hits, horns pad2x, out 2x, bubble verse 2x, same w hits, horns pad 4x, tptsolo{Gm4 D2 C2}16x clav {d f d g f d c ® c d d d f d g}, end g g-g

E.B.'s Prayer • Em • Organ Bubble / DXClavinette

Guitar & Drum intro, "See Jah Light.." w Organ 1st/3rdx hit, Xhosa verse, hits, Clav={baba baba ^5 4 3}, end clav, 1^2 ^3

Latest CD Inserts' Liner Notes

Born May 4 1655 in Padua, Venice, Italy, **Bartolomeo Cristofori** invented the pianoforte around 1700-1720. There are over 6000 working parts in the body of each piano today. Over 200 strings are required for its full range of sound. It is a percussion instrument. Whatever instrument you play, you most likely also play the piano. *It is the computer of music*. All rehearsals of any musical sections most likely use the piano if accompaniment is desired.

My piano lessons began at age 5. My first teacher taught me to "improvise classical." He also taught me that my ear was the best teacher. I have had very little formal training for performance. Still I have played in front of 10s of thousands in San Francisco Carnival & "Reggae On The River" among other large venues. Only since 2004 have I been studying classical music, so like the greatest dancer ever Nureyev, I am a latecomer to my craft.

Most people in classical music branch out into other styles of music but I "branch in." From years of accumulated knowledge of many types of song construction and form, I delve deep into the roots of classical music for its structures, wisdom and beauty.

My pianist grandmother **Claudia Ruddock-Vincent** knew of her grandfather professor **Theodore Dehon Ruddock**, and how he would "not suffer a wrong note" as they used to say, meaning he would hear everything being played! Similarly, the great orchestra leader & performer **James Brown**, during performances would yell out from the stage "I got you!" to orchestra members & then he would fine them later for their playing wrong notes because he could hear everything happening at once.

On this CD Every effort is made to play exactly what the composer intended. Tempos are as close to exactly what is on the sheet music paper without the wild fluctuations. The idea is, if you are blind, you can learn the song this way. If you wish to play along to learn the song or borrow phrases from songs this is enabled with my goal of extreme clarity and the express purpose to share the charms that the composer has buried in the songs, as in a treasure hunt..

Songs # 1 & 6 to 15 use Vincent's technique of the 1st passes (A of AA and B of BB) having no sustain pedal, the 2nd pass is sustained. #s 1, 2, 6, 7 & 9 Vincent lowers the bass 1 octave.

MW5 ©2020 Teo Vincent. Vincent's music usage includes: Liszt's "Don Sanche" for film La Roux Bonne Fair • Carmens Habanera for Carcia Lorca play "The Love of Don Perlimplin" • Vincent's Montuno Wahwah for opening videos of Talier Tumbao • Vincent's "New World" for SF Mayor's Conference • 2 Oracle In-House Multimedia works Vincent compositions • Claris/Apple In-House educational Stack soundtrack. Please visit: **Vincent4Licensing.com**

01) 04:24 Orchestral Suite No.3 in D Major, BWV 1068, II: Air in D, Adagio, **Johann Sebastian Bach**, Eisenach, Germany, Mar 21 1685 - Leipzig, Germany, Jul 28 1750

02) 05:03 Concerto for 2 Violins in D Minor, BWV 1043, II: Largo ma non tanto, JSB

03) 03:55 Magnificat in D Major, BWV 243, III: Aria, "Quia respexit," Adagio, JSB

04) 04:52 Brandenburg Concerto No.3 in G Major, BWV 1048, III: Allegro assai, "

05) 02:41 Prelude in B-Flat major, BWV 866, *Vincent rearrangement (to be more relaxing)*, **Bach & Vincent**

06) 02:56 Water Music, HWV 348, VI: Air in F Major, Presto **George Frederic Handel**, Halle, Brandenburg Feb 23 1685 – London, England Apr 14 1757

07) 01:16 Air in G minor, HWV 467, Lentement, Handel

08) 03:45 Suite, HWV 452, I: Alemende, Handel

09) 02:44 Suite in D minor, HWV 437, III: Sarabande (called "The Folia by Handel" *La Folia is by* **Corelli**), Handel

10) 06:23 Keyboard Sonata in D Minor, K.001, Giuseppe **Domenico Scarlatti**, Naples, Italy, Oct 26 1685 - Madrid, Spain, Jul 23 1757

11) 09:31 Keyboard Sonata in C Major, K.170, Scarlatti

12) 03:26 Keyboard Sonata in A Major, K.208, Scarlatti

13) 05:16 Keyboard Sonata in E Major, K.380, Scarlatti

14) 10:47 Keyboard Sonata in F Minor, K.466, Scarlatti

15) 07:00 Keyboard Sonata in E Major, K.531, Scarlatti

16) 05:31 Orfeo ed Euridice, Wq.30, II: Dance of the Blessed Spirits (Danse des Champs Elysées), Lent très dour, **Christoph Willibald Gluck**, Upper Palatinate, Germany Jul 02 1714 - Vienna, Austria Nov 15 1787

Masters' Works, 5 Classical Piano Performance CDs. This is: MWIV © 2020 Teo Vincent.

01) 3:11 Le nozze di Figaro (Marriage of Figaro), K.492, Act II, Andante con moto, Aria: Voi Che Sapete, **Wolfgang Amadeus Mozart**, Salzburg, Austria, Jan 27 1756-Dec 5 1791. His father **Leopold Mozart's** landmark book also created in 1756: "Versuch einer gründlichen Violinschule" ("The Art of the Violin").

02) 2:25 Piano Concerto No.23, K488, Adagio piano solo, **Mozart**

03) 4:07 Vesperae solennes de confessore, K.339, V. Laudate Dominum, Andante ma un poco sostenuto, **Mozart**

04) 3:25 Requim Mass in D Minor, K626, III. Sequenz 6. Lacrymosa in D Minor, **Mozart**, Completion of the work is attributed to his friend Franz Xaver Süssmayr (Schwanenstadt, Upper Austria 1766 – Vienna Sep 17 1803)

05) 2:47 Clarinet Concerto in A, *Theme Reduction*, K 622, II. Adagio, **Mozart**

06) 2:15 Symphony No.40 in G Minor, K.550, III. Minuet, Allegretto, **Mozart**

07) 2:43 Adagio in F Minor, IJS 1, Joseph Bologne, **Chevalier de Saint-Georges**, "**The Black Mozart,**" Baillif, Guadeloupe Dec 25, 1745 - Paris, France, Jun 10, 1799. Bio includes: At 17 he was made "Controller Ordinary of Wars", with the title of "Écuyer" for 11 years. Successful composers that dedicated works to him include Antonio Lolli (1764), François-Joseph Gossec (1766) and Carl Stamitz (1770). At her request, performed with Queen Marie-Antoinette at Versailles in 1779. Against slavery, he helped found the Société des amis des noirs. He was Colonel of Légion Saint-Georges an army of 1000 men in 1792, his protege, another aristocrat-African-slave-mulatto **Alexandre Dumas'** son wrote The 3 Muskateers. Orchestras he led include: Le Concert des Amateurs, Les Concert Spirituel, Orchestra at the masonic Cercle de l'Harmonie, Orchestra of the Concert de la Loge Olympique.

The Paris symphonies are a group of six symphonies written by Franz Joseph Haydn, Nos. 82-87, commissioned by the Chevalier de Saint-Georges. Haydn was to be paid 30 louis d'or for each symphony (equivalent to 1300 gulden). For more information: http://chevalierdesaintgeorges.homestead.com

08) 1:57 Dramma giocoso; Il mondo della luna (Comic Opera; "The World of the Moon"), Hob.XXVIII:7, IJH 311, Andante, Aria: "O Luna Lucente," **Franz Joseph Haydn**, Rohrau, Austria, Mar 31 1732 – May 31 1809

09) 1:14 Allegretto No.6 in E Flat Major, Royal Conservatory Piano Book, **Haydn**

10) 4:40 Piano Sonata No.8, Op.13 "Pathetique." Adagio cantabile, **Ludwig van Beethoven**, Bonn, Electorate of Cologne, a principality of the Holy Roman Empire, now Germany, Baptized Dec 17 1770 – Mar 26 1827

11) 5:44 Romance in F Major, *Vincent Reduction*, Opus 50, Adagio cantabile, **Beethoven**

12) 6:37 Piano Sonata No.1, Op.2 No.1. IV Prestisimo in F Minor, **Beethoven**. "To Joseph Haydn" who was one of his many teachers, *written on first page of the score.*

13) 1:15 Menuetto in C Sharp Minor, D600, IFS 506, Moderato, **Franz** Peter **Schubert**, Vienna, Austria Jan 31 1797-Nov 19 1828. Composed over 600 lied (songs). Was pall-bearer for Beethoven.

14) 8:14 Symphony No.8, D.759, "Unfinished." II Andentino con moto, **Shubert**

15) 3:14 4 Impromptus, D.899, II Allegro in E Flat, *Vincent Rearrangement*, Schubert

Composers are put in the order of their death dates. This shows <u>The Era</u> that they contributed to. This way when you hear the CD you are hearing the evolution of music itself.

Recordings are "Raw"–no effects. Whatever effect is desired can be added for Licenced use

MWI ©2021 Teo Vincent. Vincent's music usage includes: Liszt's "Don Sanche" for film La Roux Bonne Fair • Carmens Habanera for Carcia Lorca play "The Love of Don Perlimplin" • Vincent's Montuno Wahwah for opening videos of Talier Tumbao • Vincent's "New World" for SF Mayor's Conference • 2 Oracle In-House Multimedia works Vincent compositions • Claris/Apple In-House educational Stack soundtrack. Please visit: **Vincent4Licensing.com**

01) 3:53 O Sole Mio, **Eduardo Di Capua**, Naples, Italy, Mar 12 1865 – Oct 03 1917

02) 3:54 Gnossiennes, No.1, Lent, 1890, IES 24, Éric **Erik** Alfred Leslie **Satie**, Honfleur, France, May 17 1866 – July 1 1925, Wrote for Dadaist 391, Vanity Fair and others.

03) 3:29 3 Gymnopédies, No.1, Lent et Douloureux in D, Satie

04) 5:31 Nocturno in F Minor, IMF 9, 1896, **Manuel** Maria de los Delores **de Falla** y Matheu, Cádiz, Spain, Nov 23 1876 – Nov 14 1946, Manuel de Falla's face was on Spain's 1970 100 Pesetas Banknote.

05) 0:48 Vienna, City of My Dreams *Wien, du Stadt meiner Träume*, Opus 1, 1914, **Rudolf Sleczynski,** Polish ancestry, Vienna, Austria, Feb 23 1879 – May 5 1952

06) 2:55 Theme from *A Summer Place*, **Max**imilian Raoul **Steiner**, Vienna, Austria, May 10 1888 – Dec 28 1971

07) 4:51 Waltz in D Minor (Suite for Jazz Orchestra No.2), Op.53, 1938, **Dmitri** Dmitriyevich **Shostakovich**, Saint Petersburg, Russia, Sep 25 1906 – Aug 9 1975

08) 3:57 Cavatina (Soundtrack for *The Deer Hunter*), **Stanley Myers**, Birmingham, UK, Oct 6 1930 – Nov 9 1993

09) 5:57 Adagio Por Cordes, 1949, **Remo Giazotto**, Rome, Italy Sep 04 1910 – Aug 26 1998, University of Florence professor. Great cataloger of Albinoni & other composers. (Figured Bass by **Tomaso Albinoni** Venice, 1671)

10) 2:38 F Perfect 9ths Improvisation, **Teo** Barry **Vincent** IV, West Hollywood, California, USA, Earth, The Heavens, ∞

11) 2:43 Lilly's Song, Major-Minor-Dominant Study, Vincent

12) 1:45 B Flat Impromptu, Vincent

13) 2:26 C Major Waltz Impromptu, Vincent

14) 2:23 Fantasies on Habanera, Vincent

15) 3:32 E-Flat Nocturne Salsa, Chopin-Vincent

16) 1:08 Droplets Improvisation In D Minor, Vincent

17) 2:36 From Me & You, Composed on the day just before my son **TV V** was born! Vincent

Synthegration Soundcheck

Teo Vincent of Givnology.ca on Dual Yamaha DX-100 Synthesizers, Customized Sounds & Original, Wildly Creative Arrangements.

Vivaldi•Bach•Handel•Scarlatti
Albéniz•Debussy•da Motta•
Beethoven•Haydn•Mozart

Soundcheck means wild experiments of patches, octaves, pedals & arrangements. Short clips can be used for jingles, beds & soundtracks!

#	Time	Track
01	1:58	Vivaldi, Concerto In G Major, Andante Pizzicato, RV 532
02	1:15	Bach, Concerto for 2 Violins in D Minor, BWV 1043, Largo
03	1:45	Handel, Water Music, HWV 348, VI: Air in F Major, Presto
04	1:18	Scarlatti, Keyboard Sonata in D Minor, K.001 (1st Half)
05	2:20	Albéniz, España, Op.165, II. Tango in D Major
06	0:34	Debussy, Petit Negre Cakewalk Allegro giusto très rythmé
07	1:44	Motta, 3 Scenas Portuguezas #1, Cantiga d'Amour, Op. 9
08	1:26	Beethoven, Minuet In G, Harpsichords
09	1:15	Beethoven, Minuet In G, Orchestra Bass
10	2:39	Haydn, Sonata In A, Menuet & Trio, Hoboken XIV, No. 12
11	2:45	Haydn, Sonata In A, Menuet & Trio, Orchestra Bass
12	2:08	Nanner Mozart Notebook, Allegretto No. 41
13	5:26	Scarlatti, Sonata in E, K 380
14	0:46	Sor, Spanish Romance (with Wah-wah), IFS 85
15	4:21	Yradier/Iradier, El Arreglito, Cancion Habanera
16	1:42	Bizet, Carmen, Interlude Entr'acte "Aragonaise"
17	2:13	Mozart, Violin Concerto No. 5 in A Major, Adagio, K.219
18	1:25	Handel, Air in G minor, HWV 467, Lentement
19	3:48	Scarlatti, Keyboard Sonata in E Major, K.531
20	2:09	Scarlatti, Keyboard Sonata in A Major, K.208
21	5:21	Scarlatti, Keyboard Sonata in G Minor, K.426
22	1:27	Mozart, Violin Concerto No. 5 in A Major, Adagio, K.219
23	1:37	Sor, Spanish Romance, IFS 85
24	2:03	Yradier, El Arreglito, Cancion Habanera (Wah-wah bass!)
25	2:09	Albéniz, España, Op.165, II. Tango in D Major
26	0:51	Albéniz, España, Op.165, II. Tango in D Major, Improv's
27	5:18	Bach, Brandenburg Concerto #2 in F Andante, BWV 1047
28	1:07	Bach, Brandenburg Concerto #2 Andante, Harpsichords
29	3:53	Handel, Orchestral Suite, HWV 452, I: Alemende
30	1:16	Beethoven, Minuet In G, Orch. Bass
31	2:39	Yradier, El Arreglito, Cancion Habanera
32	2:10	Bist du bei mir, BWV 508, Bach aria, Stoölzel's Diomedes
33	0:52	Handel, Air in G minor, HWV 467, Lentement
34	1:23	Teo Vincent Wah-wah Jamming 2019 0327 "We Made It!"
35	1:20	Bach, Suite #3 in D, BWV 1068, Air, Adagio (overdone!)

All Production © Teo Vincent of Givnology.ca 2023 10 12

My 1st piano teacher Ed Bogus loaned me an electric piano, that was great. I remember an organ sound I would use sustain on it and get so lost in overlapping notes, wow I got my bad mood out then! Later I had a foot pedal pumped organ, you could hear the squeak.. At 1 point I had a Farfisa Combo Compact, a famous old sound – it had a knee controller to make it brighter! My first experience with a Hohner D6 Clavinet was (*The Monkeys'*) **Peter Tork's**, he was my piano teacher in my early teens in Venice, California. I remember buying a Wah-wah effect pedal, connecting it and having a blast!

On the Yamaha DX-100 synthesizer there is a breath controller input jack. It uses a mouthpiece to make sounds be more realistic and expressive. Instead I adapted a foot pedal into it and customized the sounds myself, making Wah-wah a feature of my own customized sounds! I have a few patches with wah-wah and I often use different 1s for left and right keyboards at the same time - 1 might have better bass and the other better top notes. Using y-jacks I have the wah-wah pedal go into both keyboards most of the time. Sometimes I have it go into only 1 keyboard. Another y-jack has the sustain pedal go into both keyboards. Sometimes I take it out of 1 or the other keyboard.

The combinations of which patch on which keyboard, whether or not the modulation / breath controller is controlled by the foot pedal and also which keyboard might have sustain pedal operating is a fun challenge! Who knows, 1 day maybe 2 wah-wah foot pedals at the same time? 2 sustain pedals too? Use them by moving knees left or right, or waving an arm or something?

Romantic Piano doesn't really belong on synthesizers, all that *piano* and *forte* meaning dynamics, that is best on the piano, so sorry, likely no Chopin on the synthesizers! Harpsichords do not have any piano or forte, so music from that era goes well on synthesizers. Forms like minuet from that era go well on them too.

Since **Latin music** - Salsa and Caribbean World Music is my specialty, I put them on synthesizers also, because I have so much tempo! Often in those cases I will have TUMBAO meaning bass patterns based on conga drum patterns in the left (bass) using staccato sounds, no sustain usually, and more sustaining sounds on the right to accent the combination of opposite sound types, therefore filling up the sonic space: *staccato and legato all at once!*

When playing music in Jazz & Calypso Trios I would sometimes read the melody and chords from a "Fake Book" or score and come up with the left hand accompaniment on the spot. Now I do that with modifying octaves to fit on these keyboards or transposing the keyboards up or down for the best combinations. I could use many more pre-programmed sounds by having the Yamaha DX-100 synthesizers play through MIDI cables and have the sounds come out of other sound units, but that is another whole project! When I do that, I can often play drum patches on both, soloing over *Guaguanco* or other basic percussion patterns, then play **drums and bass at the same time**, then bass and piano so there is another world coming when I play in that setup!

I may never decide totally on what sounds to use for songs, sometimes I want a more natural sound, sometimes a sound with a more specific effect like *tines* type of attack or slow *strings* like sustain. The keyboards have nice vibrato that I can set the delay, amount and speed of, so when I feel emotional I can amp up the wildly moody vibrations - weird vibes man! Hopefully I have been tasteful enough, playing proper sounds for the composition & style, & also wild enough to be interesting and unique. *May I let the music flow correctly, being genuine to its origins and routes.*

All Vincent's music available for licensing at Vincent4Licensing.com

Arboribus Musicorum Trees of Music • Part 2 • Page 36

Vincent's "JamBase" FileMaker Song Database

5 Songs in Year: 85

126 Shell of a Life 840900 4/4 *Ballad Dance International*
Looking at myself from outside, I see just a shell of a life, ...
  Intro: {Amin9, ®, Gmin, Fmin, Amin9}∞x Melody: {Amin, Dmin, Amin, E7 line}∞x back to intro

  Amin9

127 Fran 840600 4/4
I'm not that guy (who hurt you)

128 Must Be More To Life 840600 4/4

129 Humble Servant 840300 3/4

130 I Just Want to get to Know You 840300 4/4
Saw ya on the street the other day, ...

131 New Age Symphony 840000 4/4 *Ballad Dance Message*
A1) These are such hard times, 'nickel and dime'. These are such bad days, everyone's crazed, This is such bad news, everyone bein' used, It's such a bad scene, 'must be a bad dream - oo-oo-ooo. A2) These are such sad times, everyone into crime. These are such hard days, can't stop bein' crazed. This is such bad news, can't stop bein' used. It' such a bad scene, feels like a bad dream! oo-oo-ooo. B1) We gon'na give to you, we gon'na give you what you want. We gon'na give to you, we gonna give you what you need! 2x B2) same words - with different rhythm B3) I keep thinkin' of my Castle in the Sky! 8x
  Melody: {Emin7, A7, CMaj7, B7(+5)}∞x, Jam: {E6/9, D6/9, E6/9, A, D6/9}∞x, Outtro: {E6/9, Eb6/9, D6/9, Eb6/9}8x E6/9

  E6/9 , D6/9

6 Songs in Year: 84

132 My Fantasy 831124 4/4 *Ballad Dance Love*
I will give to you from my wishing well, everything from heaven, and nothin' from hell. My heart is open wi-de I'll give you so much you'll see, you are my everything, you're my fantasy! B: Why'd you have to be, my exact fantasy, you wilfind, you've my mind, all I beg, please be kind, with - my - mind! In my dreams, you are my favorite scene. You keep on comin' comin' comin in to my mind, so mean and so unkind(?) They say enough is enough, 3X They never witnessed your stuff 3X. You've got me hipnotized. When I see your angel eyes. B:Why'd you have to be, my exact fantasy, come what may, always stay, name your price, yes I'll pay, say - you'll - stay. C:You are the answer to all my dreams and all my desires. You are my only Earthly goal, there is no higher. You are the beautiful dream I am thinking of. You are the teacher, please grade my high, don't turn off my love because: My love is here to serve you breakfast lunch and dinner. My love is making me sing praises to your loviliness. My love is sensative to what you take and what you give. My love is begging you to - give me love back too!

133 My Lost Sweetheart 830303 3/4 *Ballad Love*
If I had known that you would brake me, I wou not have let you take me, my lost sweetheart.. I should have told myself what you'd do, I should not have left it to you, my lost sweetheart. B1) If I ever lose this pain, will it happen again? Oh I know... back to melody. additional lyrics: You gave your love that I got used to, now I need it like I used to, My lost sweetheart.
  Melody: {Cmin, Cmin/b, Cmin/bb, Cmin/a, Fmin, Dmin(-5), Bmin(-5), ab, g} Bridge: Fmin, Bb7, EbMaj7, D7(+9), Cmin9, BbMaj7, F, F/g, back

  Cmin, Cmin/b, Cmin/bb, Cmin/a, Dmin(-5), Bmin(-5), D7(+9), Cmin9

  F, F/a

| 134 C Circles | 830000 3/4 | Ballad Jazz International |

CMaj 1-6-2-5 Cmin 1-6(4)-2-5

| 135 Dream of Heaven on Earth | 830000 4/4 | |

When you feel, like you're goin' nowhere, that's exactly when you have really fight. (other) I've my life, I've my people, I've my God and my dream of heaven on earth. - repeat

| 136 Goin' on Home | 830000 3/4 | |
| 137 I Don't Have To Take This | 830000 3/4 | Ballad Message |

I don't have to take this! Oh no. You know where you can kiss. Oh yea! I don't have to take this. Oh no. I'll get back what I missed. Oh yea! B: I'm doin' what I should, and makin' my self feel good. I'm the best that I can be! I'm doin' what I should and making myself feel good. I'll be free-ee! 2nd vrse

Melody: {Cmin, Bb, Ab, Gmin, Fmin, ®, G7(+5)}4x, Bridge: Fmin, Bb7, Eb, Ab7, Fmin, Bb7, Cmin7, C7, Fmin, Bb7, Eb, Ab7, Fmin, Bb7(+9), Gmin, G7(+5), back

G7(+5) Bb7(+9)

138 I Love to Sing	830000 3/4	
139 Jerrap	830000 4/4	
140 Rock Rap	830000 4/4	Dance Fusion Message

Out on the street. Y'never can find a friend! Don't look weak, you know they will do you in! Run to the left, run to the right, anywhere to get out'a sight, better look out they're comin' fast, you better watch your head and watch your a- ...

| 141 Will I Love You | 830000 2/2 | |

CMaj

10 Songs in Year: 83

| 142 Crisp Colors | 821212 4/4 | |
| 143 Dance wit' your Clothes Off | 821205 4/4 | Ballad Dance Love |

Saw ya' in you're clothes lookin' so fine, made me think about a real good time, You know you have got me in your control. You know what I want, YOU!... bridge: Dance with your clothes off, repeat!

Melody: {{D, G, A, G}4x {C, F, G, F}, Bb, ®, A7}∞x, Jam: {{F, G, C, Bb}3x F, G, C, Bb, C, ®}

| 144 Just How Cool! | 821121 6/8 | Ballad Dance Jazz |

I'm gonna write me a story, make me a scene, I ain't holdin' back a thing. You'll see, just how cool I be! I'm gonna get me some players, show them the grooves, we doin' everything real smooth. You'll see, just how cool I be! B1: Here in my harem, my twenty women. Don't think I'll share 'em twenty's my minimum. You'll see, just how cool I be! 2nd vrse We gonna put on the makeup, turn on the light. We doin' everything just right. You'll see, just how cool I be! I'm gonna get me some players, show them the lines, we doin' everything just fine. You'll see, just how cool I be! B2:(Doctor scene) You'll see, just how cool I be! 3rd vrse, B3:(to 4/4) We gonna take off our funky blues, and pu-u-ut on our dancin' shoes. Whoa! get up to get down... (back)

Melody: {Cmin, Cmin/b, Cmin/bb, Cmin/a, Ab7, Abmin7, Db7, c line}∞x, Bridge1: c, d, eb, f, bb, c, db, eb, Abmin7, Db7, c line

Cmin Cmin/b Cmin/bb Cmin/a

Havah Nagilah in Modes:
(this way you can then play it in any key!)

{V V V V i i V-iv V} *fine*

{V V iv iv iv iv V-iv V}

i i i-iv6 i-iv6

{i-i7 VI-i} {iv6-V7 iv6}

Vø V7 i i D.C. al *fine*

Greek Modes or Scales (moods?)

Johann Wolfgang von Goethe said "Architecture is frozen music." Columns were **Doric**, then **Ionic**, then **Corinthian** (hint: each era added a syllable ☺). Our music modes system is different but similar. Yes, these were modes of music used even in Greek times. Some names are different.

Greek Mode	Roman Letter	Solfege	White Notes	Also Known As	Scale Degree	Quality
Ionian	I	Do	C to C	Major Scale	Tonic	Major
Dorian	ii	Re	D to D	Dorian Minor	Supertonic	Minor
Phrygian	iii	Mi	E to E	*Phrygian Scale*	Mediant	Minor
Lydian	IV	Fa	F to F	Lydian Major	Subdominant	Major
Mixolydian	V	So	G to G	Dominant Scale	Dominant	Dominant
Aolean	vi	La	A to A	Natural Minor	Submediant	Minor
Locrean	vii	Ti (Si)	B to B	*Locrean Scale*	Leading Note	Diminished

The following scale doesn't fit into the above list, for one thing it has the sharp 2nd or *augmented 2nd* interval.

Harmonic Minor Dominant – (Middle Eastern / Phrygian Dominant / Altered Phrygian / Freygish / Flamenco)

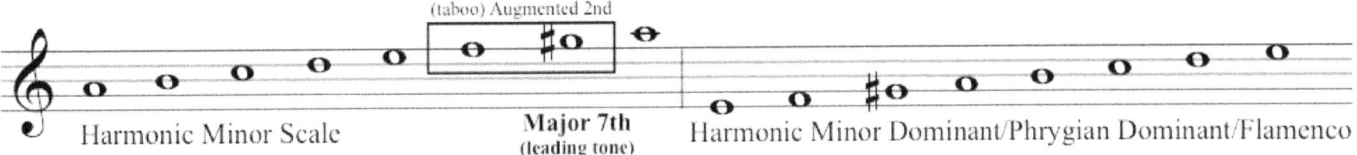

This scale is tons of fun! You'll sound like a Genie, or Andalusian Gypsy King! Play around with it!!

This song is a perfect example of this scale, do you recognize it? Make a game of who knows the song!

We are upholding traditions, sacred artistic knowledge and cultures. Hopefully you will continue keeping the art and culture alive by enjoying being another vehicle for it. ***May you enjoy carrying on the great traditions!***

Part III: Latin Music Percussion Diagrams:

Lilting melodies and beautiful harmonies are the focus of Vincent's works, but for those who wish to master expert timing and elegant dance rhythms, Afro-Latin percussion arrangements are condensed into clear and highly useful diagrams. The following are quite literally years of percussion knowledge condensed into tools and references that you can use for years to keep your tempos excellent, and to understand rhythmic balance.

Percussion instruments' names and their roles are one and the same!

The form commonly called "Salsa" a Latino would call Son or Mambo or Cha-cha.

Son & Mambo Breakdown

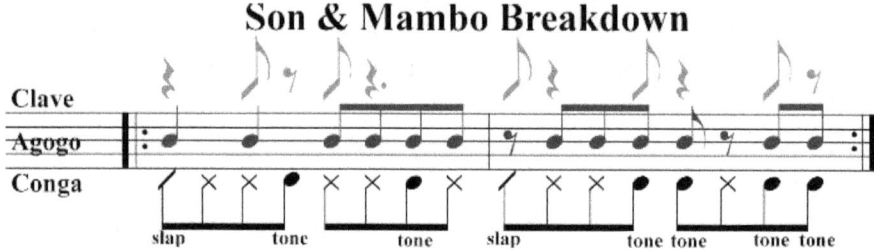

Tap the beat with your foot, focusing awareness on the pulse, and say out loud each percussion part such as **"Tap.. tone tone, tap.. to-tone.. to-tone-tap.."** until you can see it's individual logic, and how it is related to the other patterns. Eventually you can simply tap your foot in your mind.

Study clearly the interplay between the roles, the similarities, and where they accent different parts of the repeating cyclic pattern. Get an understanding of how the percussion parts work together on parts of the rhythmic tension, particularly elements such as the note just before the next bar and the note just before that.

Once you can see how the layers work together such as how the left hand or bass rhythm *("Bajo Tumbao")* is often married to the conga drum pattern, then flip the pages back and forth, look at the other percussion diagrams in this book and notice how each one has individual style in complimenting the beats and phrases. The diagrams are at best an approximation, every region will have it's own style particulars. The intention here is for the performer to understand how the parts work rhythmically together to create a whole sound, just as chordal instruments create a whole sound vertically, harmonically.

Afro-Caribbean Rumba is: 3 conga drums, claves, palitos (or wood block) and singing. Usually no tonal instruments. This section is a creative adaption of the percussionist roles and rules into melodic music parts and phrases.

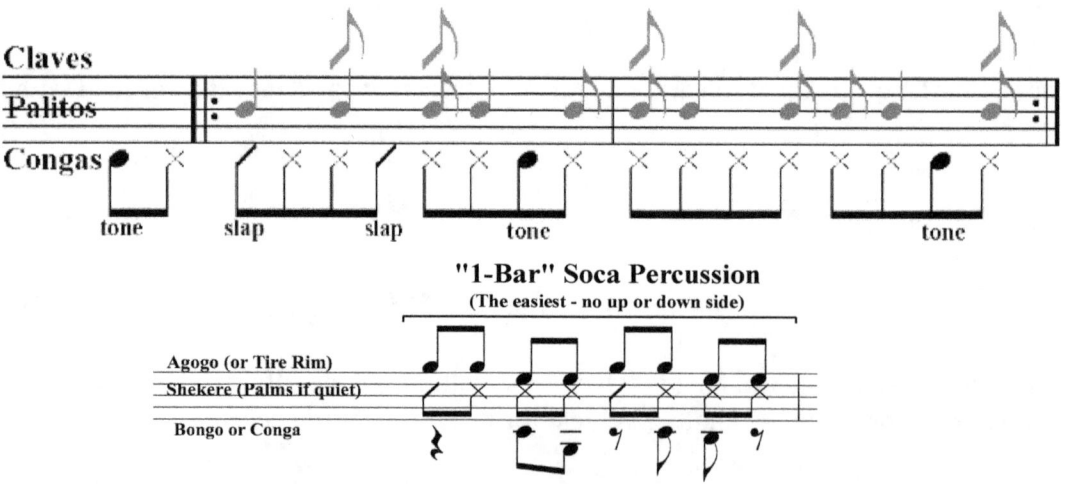

• When learning this, play it very slow, perhaps 100bpm and call it Reggae to the neighbors.

Arboribus Musicorum Trees of Music • Part 3 • Page 40

- A montuno's role is to define the rhythmic form AND the harmonic form. The play with the rhythmic tension in 4/4 is quite complex enough for most. In swing, 6/8, it is a Herculean challenge, but musically thrilling.

- The African 6/8 "Bembe Agogo" (Cowbell) pattern has the pulse (downbeat) plus Clave, use this first.

- Great percussionists imply and substitute 6/8 patterns into songs in 4/4. Try doing it with these montunos.

Percussionist Roles: Instruments' names are their roles

Overview: The musical role has the instrument's name!

Percussion instruments and their musical roles are often the same. For example, the clave is the name of the instrument, and it's pattern. Playing correct is called being "In Clave" or if you are not, someone will say: "In Clave!" In the New World, African music understanding merged with the Europeans and created new forms that didn't exist before. The amazing thing about Latin Music is that it follows percussionist, therefore African, musical rules and approaches to composition, arrangement, and ensembles. A key component of this new mixture was that skilled percussionists have many techniques that are not found in the majority of European musics.

Claves,   Conga Drums,   Shekere,   Wood Block

Some basic ground rules would be: Parts (and the people that play them) will all be on one rhythmic focus, or clave. Other parts will focus on another rhythmic tension, repeated pattern with another accent or focus. How these two groups interact, is what the composer, arranger and quality performer set up.

A main rule that is broken is the accidentally playing the other groups pattern or emphasis, and being told "turn it over!" or "turn it around!" Friendships have been stressed, parties made less fun and other un-fun

things because people don't know where their part fits in the big picture. Am I to compliment the low drum tone, or the counter-rhythm percussionist's part, or a melodic line?
It is better to know well and very clearly which side of the pattern you are supposed to be on, and who's musical toes to not step on!

Clavitos, Claves For Beginners

Clave is the key. Quite literally! That's what the word means in Spanish. The instrument is made of 2 sticks, about one foot long and one inch thick. They make the very loud click that is the metronome in salsa and Latin music, and much more. They can be likened to the instrument "Wood Block" which usually has just about the same rhythmic function; a loud, clear and obvious tempo mark that is heard even when it is not there!

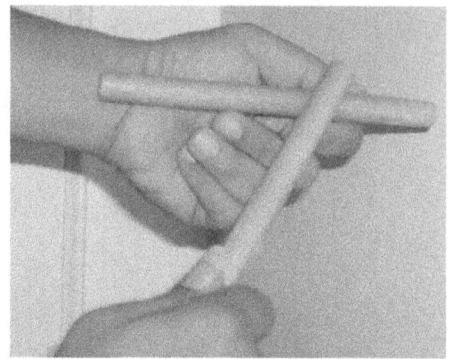

This section introduces the project of having students get used drum sticks from a drummer that they like (they are always throwing away a lot of drumsticks!), then cutting them into halves, sanding them down, optionally painting them!

The Clavitos are perfect size for beginners, and they hardly have any sound at all unless you learn exactly how to palm one, then carefully tap it in the right way with the other one.

Rumba

Drumming and dance of the poorer people from the Caribbean, particularly Cuba and Puerto Rico, mostly of African descent. No melodic instruments (usually). Conga drums with 3 specific roles: Primo=basic downbeat, Segundo=basic pattern beats, and Quinto=improvised solo, a higher tone. The 3 forms of Rumba are: Guaguanco, Columbia and Yambu. Usually includes the following percussion instruments: Claves, Palito, Shekere, sometimes Agogo (or Cowbell). <u>Each instrument has the role called by its name</u>, for example, the palito pattern could be played on something else, like the quinto, or cowbell. Since it was developed in the Caribbean, the language is Spanish, as are the melodies.

Montuno

Latin piano part, often on guitars, violins or horns. Has 2 distinct functions: 1) Usually has a "down-side" and "up-side," not always the same down side as other instruments. 2) Defines the chord progression, usually with the leading tone as the montuno's octave note (sometimes with both hands making 4 leading tones!) or the root, 3rd or 5th. Has to be rhythmically exact, and create the perfect rhythmic tension. It is a musical / tonal instrument performing a percussionist's function.

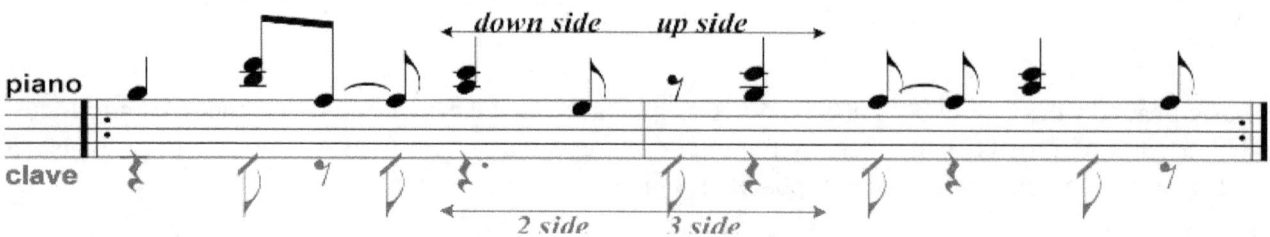

Clave Offenders

Since the most common problem is playing on the wrong side of clave, we will focus on those areas to keep you from being a clave offender. Notice from the graphic below how the Segundo conga part focuses on the beginning of bar one. It's three beats are at the beginning, it is called "in 3-2 clave." The clave part, though, focuses on the other bar, in the first bar there are only the 2 notes! It is "in 2-3 clave." The palito part, and shaker parts, should be "on the same side."

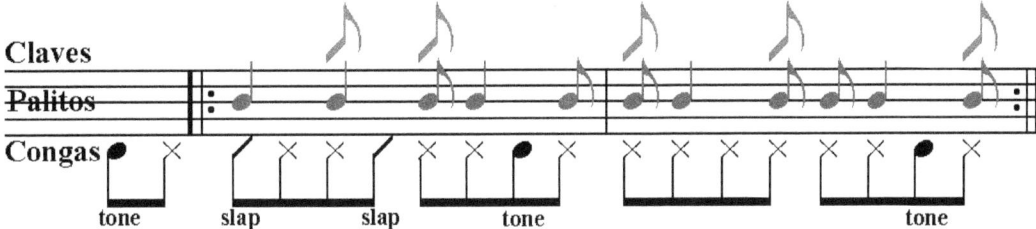

Percs1: Da-dada-da-da

What is the answer to "Da dada da da?" Let them guess for a while, and make it fun. No, it is not Morse Code, though it looks exactly like it. The answer is "Da Da!" which is the ending of many songs, symphonies and sonatas as well. Like the last 2 notes: Ta-da!

This is "Call and Response" that is famously in African music, percussion, and so many styles of music.

Also Solo and Chorus very often (and beautifully) do trade offs, "rounds" are like this as well..

This lesson's focus is that there is a "call" side of clave, and an "answer" side. The answer side is downbeats.

Have half of the students all do the **Call** part. Have the other half do the **Answer**.

Try other phrases that are designed as clave patterns:

"Shave and a haircut, two bits."

One phrase that we've designed that is very positive is in clave pattern as well:

"Peace ease and clarity, for me."

Percs2: Clave Down!

This graphic gives you a very clear demonstration of where the clave beats are in relation to the downbeat. The claves are the clapping hands images, the downbeat is the tapping foot image.

1	2	3	**4**	**5**	6	7	8	**9**	10	**11**	12	**13**	14	15	16
👏			👏	👏				👏		👏		👏			
👟				👟				👟				👟			

You can look at the clave pattern as 16 16th notes, making one bar, or 2 bars of 8th notes. A fast song usually is thought to have a "2 Bar Clave" and that is the best way for you to understand it. One bar – or side – has 3 pulses, the other bar has 3 pulses.

The above graphic is called a "3 – 2 Clave" and you can clearly see why. Sometimes you will think of the clave pattern "upside town" or "turned over" or "turned around," and that will be a "2 – 3 Clave."

First, get familiar with playing the clave and tapping the beat with your foot.

Next, be able to play the clave on a table or your leg in one hand and the pulse or beat in the other. Switch hands too!

Finally, be able to play the clave without playing the downbeat, or playing the beat in your mind only.

Listen to songs and play the clave pattern along with the song! See if you can stretch and slow down to make twice as many claves, or less longer claves. A clave can even be ½ bar, or 4 bars! Try it!

Percs3: Son Clave + Pulse

If you are not familiar with music notation, try counting the units such as: 3, 3, 4, 2, 4.

This is one way to write a one bar clave, there are others but this will do. The following is written in 2 bars, and includes the downbeat on Agogo or Cowbell.
The pulse or downbeat should be in your mind, but you can play it as well if you like.

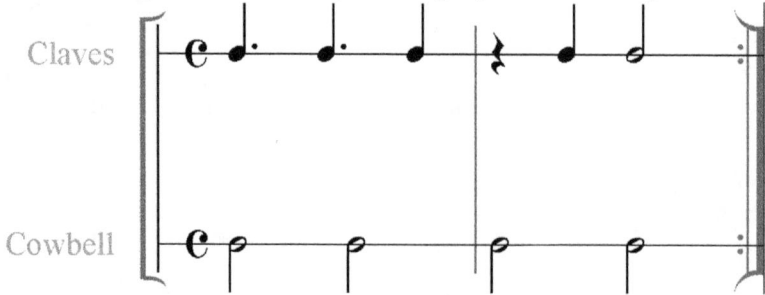

The "2 side" of the pattern is the "Down Side." It has more downbeats, and the down beat is pronounced. A "2-3" pattern has the down beat first, or the down beat side first.

Once you are playing the pattern, it will sound exactly the same, whether or not it is 2-3 or 3-2 **to you**. It **is** exactly the same to you, but in the overall arrangement it couldn't be more different.

Percs4: Palito (Simple and Basic)

Again, just like the clave pattern is named after the instrument, the palito pattern or little stick pattern mean the same thing.

This is the simple – **one bar palito**:

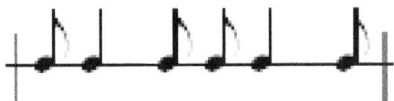

In fact, you can see that it is a 2 beat pattern repeated.

This is the basic **2 bar palito**:

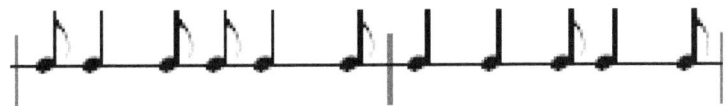

Look carefully, surely you can see which side or bar is the 2 side, meaning which is the **DOWNBEAT** side. Once you can see in that palito pattern which side is the down side, you know where the clave goes.

This palito is common in many percussionist styles, including Brazilian, Calypso, Salsa and even Boleros – ballads. It is very nice to play by simply rubbing your palms together!

Once you can play these palitos with either hand, using various fingers, it is infectious! You will find yourself tapping really nice palitos almost anytime. Keep note of which side is the down side!

You may want to end your palitos playing with the "Da da!" we learned before, think of it as the flamenco dancers last move, hand goes up gracefully. Ole!

Percs5: Clave & Palito in Binary (back and forth)

In the following example, the downbeat pattern stops for the palito part which is played with two hands.

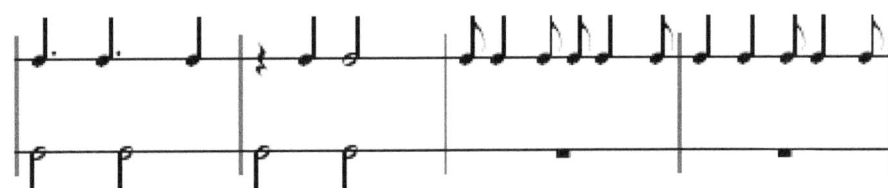

"Binary" means that you play one part for a certain amount, then the next part, back and forth.
A good idea is 4 claves, then 4 palitos, back and forth. The trick is: don't play the last little leading note of the palito pattern! It's only necessary when going back into palitos, it's not necessary for the ending, or going into the clave part again.

Percs6: Rumba Clave, Palito & Binary

Sides – claves against each other

The advanced clave is the **"Rumba Clave"** which is very similar yet very very different.

It's count is 3, 4, 3, 2, 4. The key is that the 3rd note, or "gulp," is ever so close to the 2nd half of the pattern! It is like an impossibly close note, just barely in front of the 2nd part of the pattern, and it need be accurate!

The easiest way to start learning this is to play the downbeat of the 2nd half at the same time. You can play it either with the clave pattern, or with your other hand on another instrument like a cowbell.

Eventually you can play this super-complex yet super-simple pattern without the downbeat and keep it super-tight!

Percs7: Rumba Palito

The following translation of percussion into melodic parts includes 2 opposing claves.

You will find that the Congas (Bass notes) sounds like a 3 – 2 Son Clave pattern, in opposition to the Rumba Clave.

Percs8: Rumba Clave & Rumba Palito in Binary

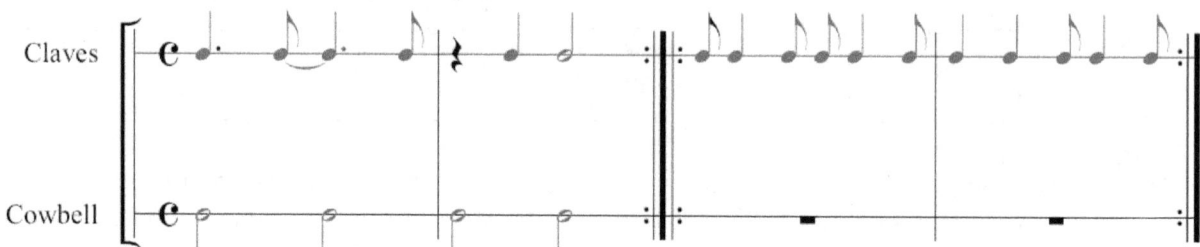

This complex Rumba Clave is similar to Son Clave but so much more exciting and fun!

"Binary" means that you play one part for a certain amount, then the next part, back and forth.

The following more advanced "Rumba Palito" should be learned after getting the basic one tight.

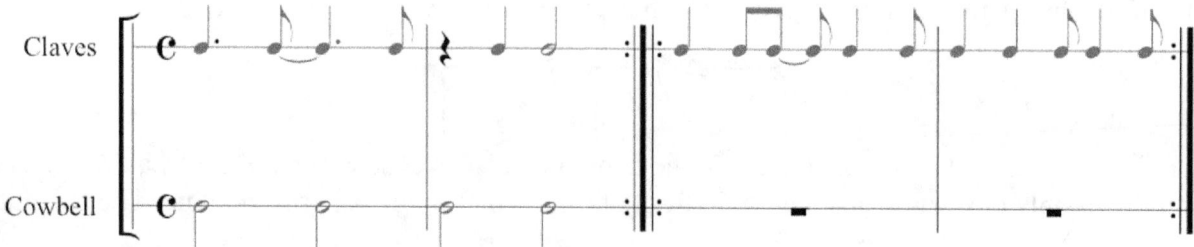

A good idea is 4 claves, then 4 palitos, back and forth.

The trick is: when going back to clave, don't play the last little leading note of the palito pattern. You may want to play it when going in to palitos.

It's only necessary when repeating palitos, it's not necessary for the ending, or going into the clave part again.

Percs9: Rumba Palito in 2-3 and Conga Dance

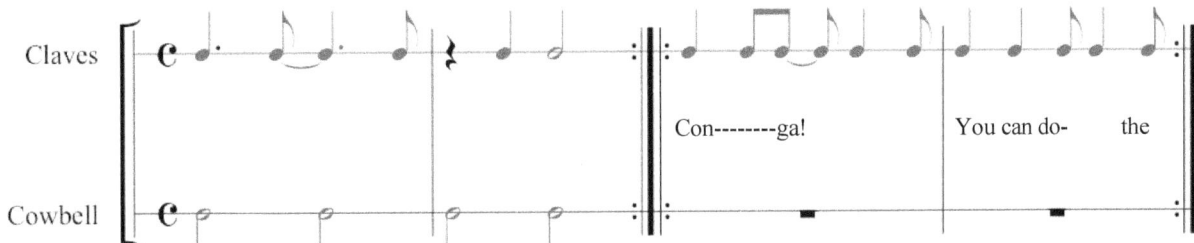

Repeat the 2nd phrase, the "Rumba Palito" by itself, but leave out the last 2 notes of the first bar.

After a while, reverse it, start on the 2nd bar.

A fun text for this is:

> **"You can do the conga**
>
> **Everyone loves the conga**
>
> **You can do the conga**
>
> **Come and dance my conga!"**

The word **conga** is the first two clave beats in the second bar. In other words the words go:

$$1 - 2 - 3 - 4 - 1 \text{ —and!}$$

Every other phrase can be improvised as well, allowing call and response!

Percs10: 6/8 Agogo & Cowbell Patterns

All of these patterns so far are in 4/4 time. The deeper African rhythms are in 6/8 (also called 12). There are 2 primary patterns played on **Agogo** bell, or in the new world, the **Cowbell**.

Syncopated Agogo Pattern

After understanding the 5 note clave, you will eventually see that those 5 notes are a subset, an abbreviation of much more complicated 7 note agogo patterns.

These are synchronized with the musical scales, the Do-Re-Mi of music in an amazing fashion. The octave is devided into 12ths, there are 12 actual notes between C and C. Of these 12 we use 7 for our scale, the 8th being the note repeated an octave away. When you play the major scale you are using whole steps and half steps. Between C and D is a whole step, but between F and G is a half step.

The Major scale is: Whole whole half whole whole whole half which if you look at the syncopated agogo pattern, is the same. The Lydian scale is: Whole whole whole half whole whole half which is the same as the downbeat agogo pattern above.

Percs20: Entries – "Counting In" With Sides

If the song is in 2 – 3 clave then the clave player – and the other instruments in sync with the clave such as the palitos, shekere and so on – will need to know how to start on the 2 side of the pattern.

Since you have been practicing both 2 – 3 and 3 – 2 patterns, it shouldn't be very difficult for you to come in either way.

Take an obvious 3 – 2 song, and count in to the song with clave and percussion

Take an obvious 2 – 3 song – probably a Rumba – count in and see the difference.

The part sounds the same, even though they are completely opposite. Funny how it is the same, and completely different at the same time hum?

Percs21: Endings – Outtros in Unison

There need be a lot of eye contact to do endings or **outtros** together, and well. The person counting will need to be ahead of everyone else, and know when to get their attention but not too soon, and definitely not too late! Then he or she should be able to let everyone know how long until the ending.

Often people will end on the clave part all together. This excerpt is from Carmen:

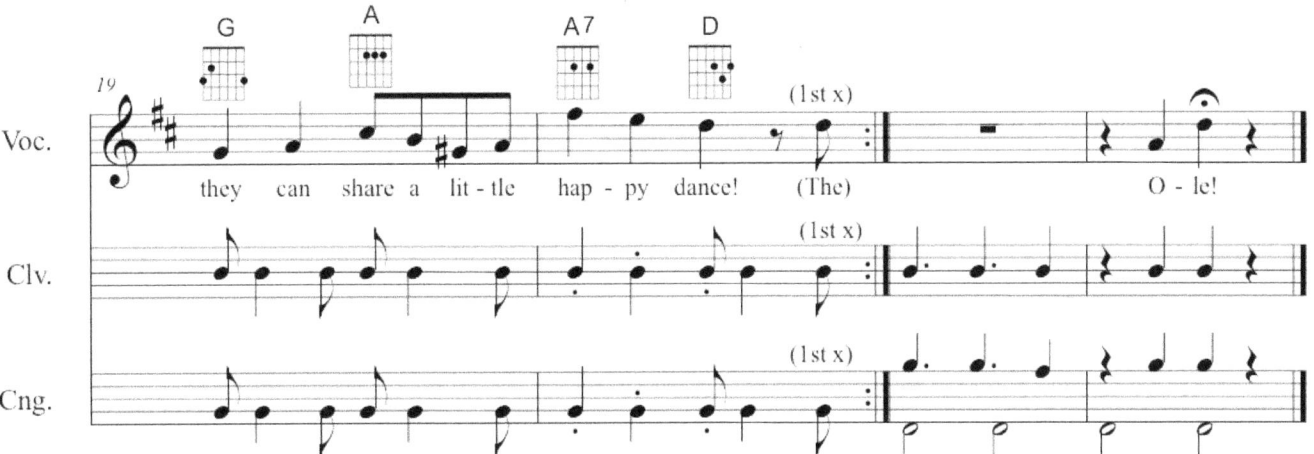

Here is a common percussion ending from Brazilian music. This is great to have the whole group do together:

Brazilian Unison Outtro

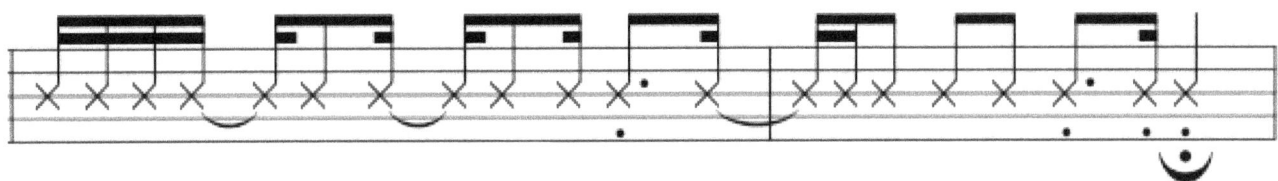

Percs22: Hearing Songs' Claves & Sides

Now when you hear a song you like, try playing various clave patterns and see which fits best! Then you can add the other parts such as palito, agogo, and perhaps even the conga drum parts.

Most songs will not have the opposing-claves technique, so don't worry about that. As far as pop or simple songs go, don't worry about being on the side of one percussion section or another, it can be considered all one unified rhythmic section.

World Music Stories

Salsa is Spanish and West African (mostly). Funny the Spanish already had an African influence from the Moors. It used the Middle Eastern Scale and interestingly, this scale *is not* West African like the rhythms of Salsa are.

Percussion Patterns Made into Melodic Phrases

In the following song the Shekere pattern is turned into the piano montuno. It is a one-bar-pattern, the simplest way to do a montuno, and there is no wrong side to it. It is more of a Cha-cha-cha montuno.

Montuno Circles Makes Blues Scale

Moderato tranquillo
♩ = 100
Piano

syncopated yet flowing

Dm11 — G7 — CΔ(add9) — FΔ(add6)
Slow Cha Cha Cha
II — V — I — IV

Bm11 — E7 — Am11 — D7 — Em11 — A7
Blues Scale occurs automatically when **double-time walking VI-II-III-VI**
VII — III — VI — II — III — VI

©2008 11 17
Teo Vincent 4th

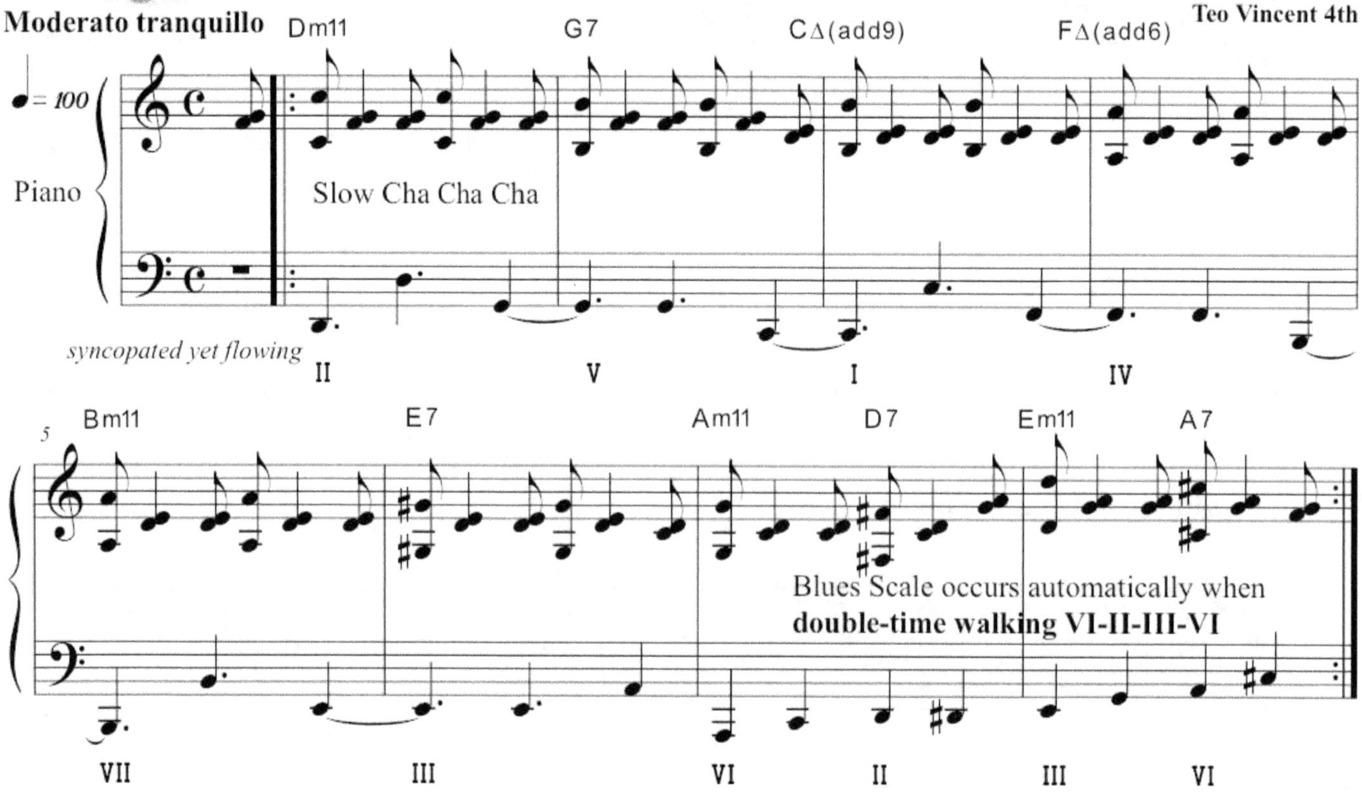

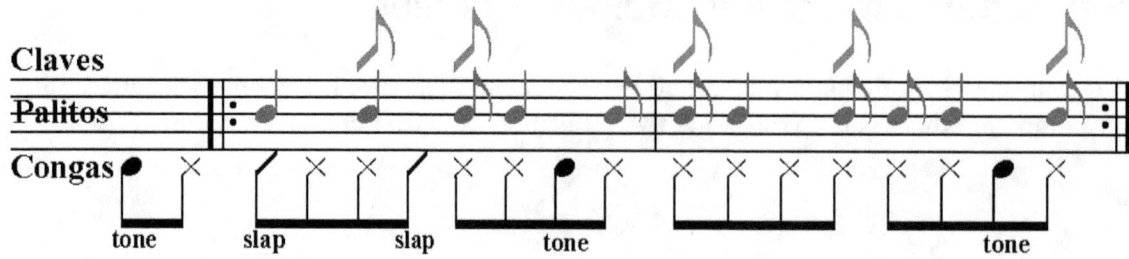

Clave Offenders

Since the most common problem is playing on the wrong side of clave, we will focus on those areas to keep you from being a clave offender. Notice from the graphic below how the Segundo conga part focuses on the beginning of bar one. It's three beats are at the beginning, it is called "in 3-2 clave." The clave part, though, focuses on the other bar, in the first bar there are only the 2 notes! It is "in 2-3 clave." **The palito part, and shaker parts, should be "on the same side."**

Claves
Palitos
Congas
tone — slap — slap — tone — tone

Arboribus Musicorum *Trees of Music* • Part 3 • Page 50

Part IV

World Music Mastery, Building Blocks for Playing With Anyone!

* Quarter tied to eighth note is more correct. ** Bass can be 1-3-5 as in bar 1 or 1-5-1 as in bar 15.

Start with just the left hand, soon you will see and know how a chord is 1-3-5 and how to make the common ones.

Notice the ROMAN NUMBERS for each chord. Lower case are minor. A "Progression" is a set of chords. You should be able to play I-IV-V in any key, as in these examples. Also i-iv-V=minor. Continue on your own up chromatic as the last three staves/staffs here do. The next is iv-i-V-i in C minor, then C# minor. Notice with these that go iv-i-V-I, f you start on the 4th bar it is i-iv-i-V! Songs can shift like this in the middle! Learn every key.

Latin Piano (Montuno) 101: "La Bamba"
C I-IV-V-IV major and minor (with I-ii-V-ii variation) *learn in all keys*

World Music Definitions of Afro-Latin Music Percussion Roles & Rules

Bembe: a religious event of the Nigerian Yoruba people. Drummers play 3 Batá drums. Batá have 2 drum heads. Each of the three drums has very specific roles. There are also usually agogo (or cowbell) patterns, shekere (or shaker) patterns, and clave patterns.

Cha-cha or Cha cha cha: slower Latin Music, also: the sound the feet make on 3-4-1 beats.

Clave: 1) wooden sticks held in a specific way to get good tone, 2) a rhythmic tension pattern, usually 5 hits. A seeming simple but quite complicated rhythmic pattern repeated endlessly. Must be accurate! One might say about your musical part: "You are not in clave!" which means that the part you are playing does not go well with clave (the montuno down side should not be on the down side of clave, see Montuno).

Diaspora: Cultural legacy. Where the peoples have traveled and influenced with their culture.

Floriano (flowery) instead of sparse parts, more notes are played, flowing.

Latin Music: from "Latin America," or Spanish-America, Cuba, Puerto Rico, the Dominican Republic, Peru, Chile, Mexico, etc.. Also called Salsa, Son or Mambo.

Mambo: 1) the style we usually call Latin Music. 2) a section of a song near the end, repeated.

Montuno: Latin piano part, often on guitars, violins or horns. Has 2 distinct functions: 1) Usually has a "down-side" and "up-side," not always the same down side as other instruments. 2) Defines the chord progression, usually with the leading tone as the montuno's octave note (sometimes with both hands making 4 leading tones!) or the root, 3rd or 5th. It has to be rhythmically exact, and create the perfect rhythmic tension. It is a musical / tonal instrument performing a percussionist's function.

Orìshás: Nigerian Yorùbá tribe's sacred deities.

Rumba: Drumming and dance form of the poorer people from the Caribbean, particularly Cuba and Puerto Rico, mostly of African descent. Usually with no melodic instruments. Conga drums with 3 specific roles:

Primo=basic downbeat, Segundo=basic pattern beats, and Quinto=improvised solo, a higher tone. **The 3 forms of Rumba are: Guaguanco, Columbia and Yambu.** Usually includes the following percussion instruments: Claves, Palito, Shekere, sometimes Agogo (or Cowbell). Each instrument has the role called by its name, for example, the palito pattern could be played on something else, like the quinto, or cowbell. Since it was developed in the Caribbean, the language is Spanish, as are the melodies.

Salsa Romantica: A more slow-dancing Latin Music, flowing. Often love songs.

Son: the style we usually call Latin Music.

Yemaya (Yemonja): The Ocean Goddess. "The Mother of the Children of Fishes." One of the Orìshás, the Nigerian Yorùbá tribe's sacred deities. She is the ultimate symbol, the personification of motherhood.

Yoruba (Yorùbá): The largest tribe in Africa, from the Lagos area of Nigeria. Most American slaves came from there. The language is a tonal language with low, mid and high tones: Yo=mid, rù=low, bá=high. In some ways, the Yoruba culture is said to be most alive in pockets of ex-slaves such as Brazil, Cuba and certain regions of the U.S. These regions are called "the Yoruba Diaspora."

https://meaning.assurances.gov.gh/orisha-colors-and-meaning.html

	Red	Orange	Yellow	Green	Blue	Indigo	Violet
Basics	Warming, Stimulating, Activating, Motivating			Neutral	Cooling - Calming, Soothing, Relaxing		
Gland	Ovaries or testes	Pancreas, spleen	Adrenals	Thymus	Thyroid	Pituitary	Pineal
Organs	Female-Uterus, vagina Male - Prostate, penis	Kidney, intestines, bladder, rectum	Stomach, liver, gall bladder	Heart	Mouth, lungs, throat	Eyes, ears	Brain
System	Reproductive	Elimination	Digestion	Circulatory	Respritory	Autonomic Nervous	Central Nervous
Location	Base of spine	Abdomen	Navel	Chest	Throat	Forehead	Top of Head
Plexus	Coccygeal	Sacral	Solar	Heart	Cervical	Medulla Oblongata	Cerebral Cortex
Musical Note	C - Do	D - Re	E - Me	F - Fa	G - So	A - La	B - Te
Fragrance	Sandalwood	Orange	Lemon	Lime	Blueberry	Plum	Violet
Gemstone	Ruby, coral, garnet	Topaz, amber	Citrine, gold	Emerald, turquoise	Sapphire, lapis	Soldalite, Azurite	Amethyst
Complimentary Color	Blue	Blue/Violet	Violet	Magenta	Red	Yellow/Orange	Yellow
Foods	Strawberries, cherries	Peaches, oranges	Corn, lemons	Lettuce, spinach	Blueberries, plums	Blue & Violet foods	Purple grapes
Lessons	Self-awareness, Base Instincts, Procreation	Social issues, Herding Instinct, Self-sufficiency	Intellect, Personal power, Analysis	Unconditional Love, Non-attachment, Balance, Security	Communication, Creativity, Live in moment, Inner Peace, Free Will	Develop Intuition, Wisdom, Truth	Spiritual Connection, Manifestation, Imagination, Grounding, Humility, Focus
Gift	Lust for Life	Social Interaction	Intellect	Clairsentience	Clairaudience	Clairvoyance	All Psychic Senses

The following song at page 3 cleverly includes advanced translating of percussion parts into melodic phrases.

Yorùbá Diasporas (page 2)

"Rumba"
"Palito" (the word means little sticks) wood block patterns turned into piano "montuno" phrase

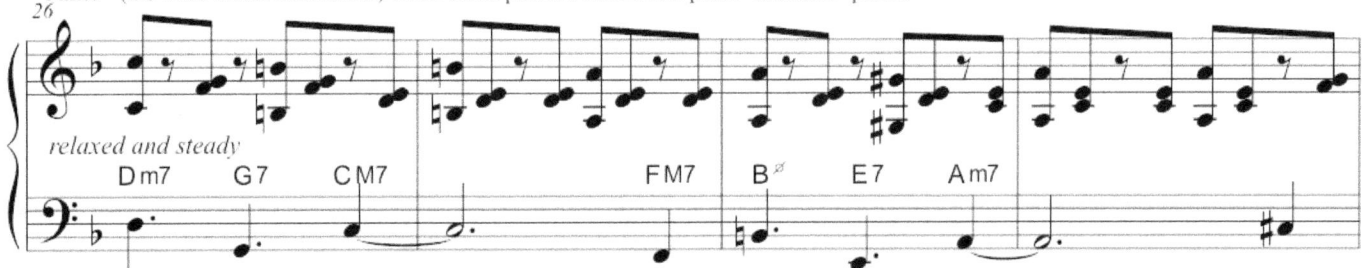

relaxed and steady

"Segundo" drum part. The foundation of Rumba is the "Tres Golpes" of the segundo opposite the "3 side" of the rumba clave pattern

Too hot and spicy? Skip to next pepper

Afro-Caribbean Rumba is: 3 conga drums, claves, palitos (or wood block) and singing. Usually no tonal instruments. This section is a creative adaption of the percussionist roles and rules into melodic music parts and phrases.

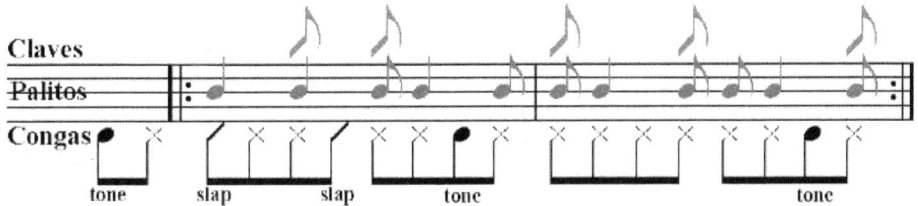

Yorùbá Diasporas (page 3)

"Rumba Clave" especially complex syncopation pattern played expressively on chromatic dissonant chords

"Rumba Palito" a more syncopated little sticks (wood block) pattern re-envisioned into a tasty piano montuno

Yorùbá Diasporas (page 4)

Chromatic Montuno #1

Chromatic Montuno #2

Arboribus Musicorum *Trees of Music* • Part 4 • Page 57

Yorùbá Diasporas (page 5)

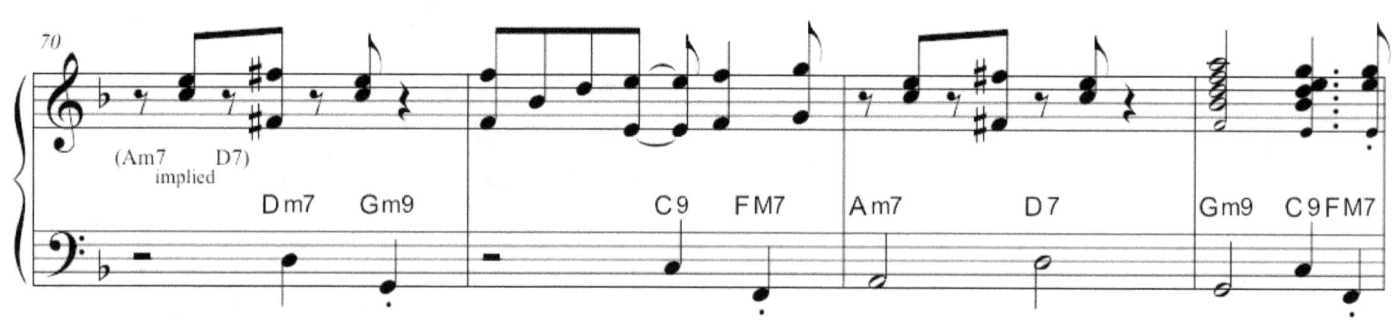

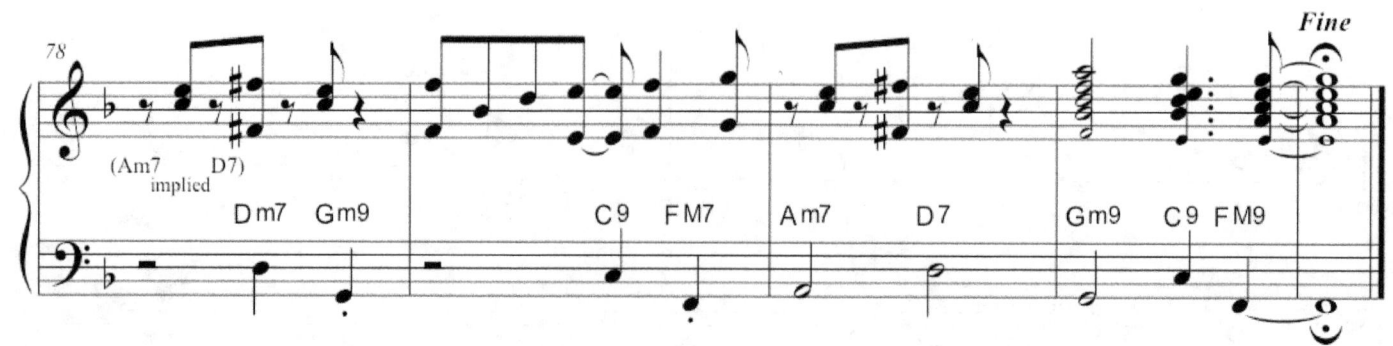

Complimenting Ensembles

One of the most advanced business techniques is to groom your successor. Rather than just keep your competition down, you help the person that will replace you, so that you move up the ladder.

The pianist's role is often to accompany the singer. By extension, the keyboardist is often giving everybody in the ensemble their part, harmonic structure, tempo and even feel or mood. In the old operas the harpsichord might be so quiet that it is drowned out by the louder instruments, but it's role is key to keeping the orchestra "in the groove."

In Jazz, the term is: The Piano **Comps**. Comping in another way of looking at it is playing the accompaniment. Comp chords are giving the harmonic structure to the basic melody and parts.

There are many reasons why an artist compliments his friends a lot: for one, if one is judged by the company that they keep, then showing their company in the best view is best for them as well! It is also just simply good to encourage the best in people, help them see their accomplishments and good points rather than focus on their weaknesses. I remember being absolutely wowed by Pat Metheny's keyboardist Lyle Wagner, but he was more the backbone, in the shadows, allowing the star to shine ever so brightly. Lyle is great at complimenting, in the best sense of the word, and the best sense of the work.

When all the parts of the ensemble are clear on the overall structure and process throughout a song, having the conductor inside each musician keeping each in their proper role and compliment to the whole, this is when everything flows gracefully and beautifully.

Highlife has: 1-Rhythm, 2-Line and 3-Lead Guitar Parts

Highlife is a beautiful and fun the West African style of dance music.

Highlife style was made popular by King Sunny Ade the great guitarist among others.

One guitar plays chords. Another plays "the line," an important part of the arrangement rhythmically *and* harmonically. The third guitar is the lead guitarist, and the lead part may be a 8 bar phrase or even longer!

Afrobeat was an important synthesis of the two: Nigerian and American Soul musics by the famous Nigerian artist **Fela Kuti**. Fela was very inspired by the American James Brown's Soul Music and guitar grooves so Afrobeat was a way of merging old and new styles.

The great Camaroonian composer Hugh Masakela did similarly with "Soul Makosa," a song popular in the 1970s. Makosa is a traditional African musical form.

Many African musicians came to California originally on tour with Hugh Masakela's band in the 1970s.

Some musicians came to California from playing with Fela. His son still leads his band.

There is a Cameroonian band that plays awesome salsa, and sings in Spanish, and doesn't even know what they are saying! Their tempos are amazingly tight though! What goes around, comes around!

Calypso Study for Duet

© 2009
Teo Vincent 4th

Presto giocoso - quick & playful ♩ = 200

Soloist

Keyboard

Fast Soca (Soul-Calypso)

One Bar Calypso Percussion

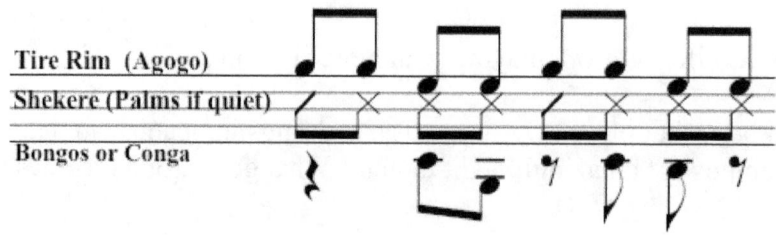

The one bar pattern has no down side and up side. The following two bar patterns do have up and down sides:

Two Bar Soca (Soul-Calypso) Percussions

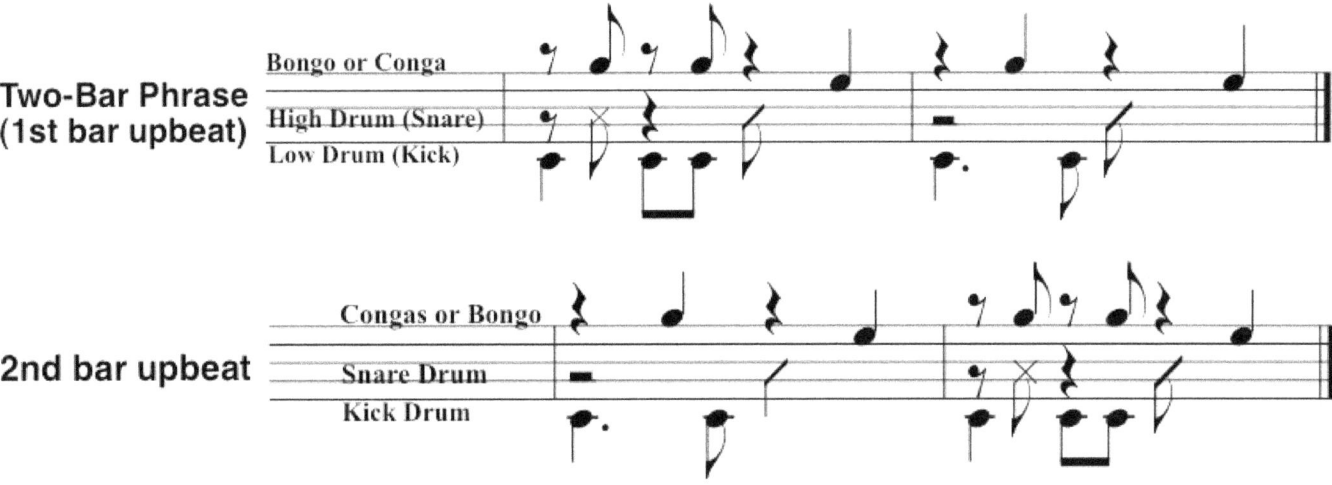

Have one person play both the low and high drum parts, repeated, and then another person come in with the bongo drum part. These things can also be sung instead of played on drums.

The kick and snare could sound like: "Boo – pootat, Bootaboopootat." The next part could be sounded like "bing, bong, bingbing, bong."

Then reverse the patterns: The kick and snare are: "Bootaboopootat, Boo – pootat" and the bongo is: "bingbing, bong, bing, bong."

After trying the above examples, you can see clearly that one side is up and another is down. This helps immensely as you coordinate the group to play and sound good together.

Can you see that just like a clave pattern, both of the two bar patterns are identical except for where they start?

Rhythm Section Accompaniment "Chucks"

Notice how the piano part and guitar chords have accent on the first beat – by following it immediately, not at all like the 2nd half extremely on-the-beat. We can assume therefore, that their "down" side is the 2nd half, in other words, the accompaniment to Calypso Study #1 is in "3-2 clave."

Also notice that the melody highlights the clave pattern on the second side, as Jazz chords often do. Unlike the accompaniment, the melody is clearly in a phrase that is in "2-3 clave." This combination means that the musicians don't step on each other's foot, they leave the all important spaces!

The guitar to be right after the 1 is a special Soca (Soul-Calypso) technique that makes the rhythm very bouncy, well, how else could Trinidadians, "Trinys," win so many carnival competitions? To dance for hours with heavy costumes and such, special bouncy Soca "Guitsy Riddim" keeps you up (and up beat)!!

The Yoruba People from Nigeria, West Africa

To be totally correct it is actually Yorùbá: The largest tribe in Africa, from the Lagos area of Nigeria. The Yoruba are the most traveled around the world historically. The majority of American slaves came from there. The language Yorùbá is a tonal language, low mid and high tones: Yo=mid, rù=low, bá=high.

In some ways, the Yoruba culture is said to be most alive in pockets of ex-slaves such as Brazil, Cuba and certain regions of the U.S. These are called "the Yoruba Diaspora."

Some Afro-Latin Music definitions:

Latin America basically means Spanish America: Cuba, Puerto Rico, the Dominican Republic, Panama, Argentina, Columbian, Nicaragua, El Salvador, Peru, Chile, Guatemala, Mexico, etc.. mostly Catholic cultures.

Latin Music is from Latin America. It is also called Salsa, Cha-cha, Son or Mambo. Although it is a long distance, both physically and culturally, the rhythm in Latin Music is or has African roots. Latinos all know this, and they are quite proud of the African drums and culture mixed into their music.

Sadly, people in the United States often don't know how rich Latin music is with deeply loved African roots. This is partly because under slavery in the US drums were illegal, as was speaking any African language or doing things resembling African culture – though in some rare cases some survived.

A ***Bembe*** is a religious event of the Nigerian Yoruba people. Drummers play 3 Batá drums. Batá are sacred drums that have 2 drum heads. Each of the three drums has very specific roles. Other percussion instruments are often agogo (or cowbell) patterns, shekere (or shaker) patterns, and clave patterns.

Songs are to honor their deities called "**Orishas**." Sometimes they (and the religion itself) are called "The Seven Powers," though there are many orishas and they have wonderfully interesting stories and interactions with each other! Chango is the warrior and lover. Yemaya the ocean goddess. Osain the owner of herbs. Ochossi is the hunter. Ogun rules metals. Elegbara (or Elegua or Eshu) is the trickster. Oya the wild woman of the cemeteries. Ochun the Love Goddess. Others are: Orunmila the owner of the divination system or "Table of Ifa," Obatala the ruler of the head, Orunmila Goddess of the Heavens, Ibeji The Twins.

They have been "syncretized" with the Catholic Saints. Chango is Santa Barbara (both have the colors red and white), Niño de Atocha is Eshu, Virgin de Caridad del Cobre is Oshun, etc.. This way the followers could pray to Chango but tell master that they were praying to Santa Barbara.

This Nigerian language and culture in the new world is called "**Lukumi**" which is a word in the Yoruba language which means "friend." This is simply to distinguish it from it's Nigerian roots. This culture is quite alive and vibrant in many parts of the new world. See the movie **"Quilombo"** about Brazilian escaped slaves to see good examples of the Yoruba Orishas / Dieties.

The integration of the roots of salsa – Nigerian Yoruba tribe's music – into modern, new world music, is a thrilling blend of old and new, earthy and sophisticated, tribal and social, that is immensely entertaining and also greatly educational and uplifting for many people who have lost the connection with their roots.

The Jazz Standard **"Afro-Blue" by Mongo Santamaria is an Orisha song to Obatala.** Orishas are deities or Gods of the Yoruba tribe (largest tribe in Africa) in Nigeria. In Latin America the religion of the Yoruba (often called Lukumí here in the New World) commonly called Santaría, Siete Potencias or 7 Powers. The

USA has very little knowledge of Orisha songs. Oba-king Tala-head; Obatala is a great Orisha, and there are recordings of the song sung by Babalawos or priests, though of course the one we know is modified.

First, the melody of "Afro Blue" only shares the first few pitches with the ocha song for Obatala with text "Iyalawka orisha-o, iyalakwa akaki oke. It has been adapted & converted to African-American popular, non-religious, *secular music.*

Motifs and Motivations

Pianist Anton Kwerti in a lecture at The Royal Conservatory of Music was talking about Beethoven's 5th Piano Concerto: "Beethoven used the Salami style of composing. He chops the motif into little pieces like a salami, and you want to pick up the pieces off of the floor."

The "word" in music is the motif. Put them together and you get sentences, paragraphs etc.. You may read it as *motif* in one book, *motive* in another, they are the same thing! In LVB's 5th Symphony we have the classic motif of S-S-S-L-- (short short short long), perhaps the most well known motif of all (It was written just as he was losing his hearing and some think it is "I can not **hear!**" or "Why make me **deaf?!**"). If we expand the motif to s-s-s-l-s-l-s-l then we get a phrase that begs an answer. It motivates you to reply.

Beethoven't 5th becomes a Perpetual Motivator

Call and Response / Rhythmic Balance in Latin Music

The **"Tumbau,"** the rhythm that dancers so love in Latin Music of Bass & Montuno is Rhythmic Counterbalance. The accented quarter note in the left hand with the eighth note accent in the right hand is extremely complex and difficult even for virtuoso classical pianists (bar 5 of "Montuno Etude" in a few pages).

An excellent exercise for the whole group is the beautiful fun song: *Sandungera* by the group *Los Van Van*.

Calypso and Zouk styles of music often have the bass guitar accent the 3 and 4 of the phrase. If you listen to West African Highlife, you will often hear this same accent.

What African and African rooted music gives you is the rhythmic tension that makes you want to hear the completion of the pattern, the answer, musically, rhythmically.

In addition to the magic of beats of rhythm propelling you up to dance and sing, the beauty and grace of masterful music played by energetic and vibrant performers motivates you to share your own beauty and grace with the world. Get inspired and get involved in motivating music!

Afro-American Contributions

"Latin Music" is Black Man's heritage. Latinos know that it is African rhythms in their music. Even so African that it throws you off, you are lost unless you really know it, like traditional complex African music.

In the U.S. drums was illegal. They thought the slaves could communicate and plan revolts. African music and culture was thoroughly removed! What is suppressed, repressed and held back re-emerges. *"What you resist persists!"* Inevitably the African sense of rhythm and it's divinity naturally arose in Afro-American culture.

Louisiana was French - blacks could play drums in "Congo Square" on Sundays. This is one reason why so much of Afro-American music is from New Orleans, Louisiana.

1st Contribution-> Singing & soul wrenching excitement, even possession by (the holy) spirit inserted into the black Baptist church.

2nd Contribution-> Drum balance re-emerging generations later. The Rhythmic Tension of drum parts re-invented and evolved. Drums made into harmonic, melodic musical parts and phrases. Sections arranged as if they were percussion sections or following percussionist rules.

Play the rhythm 3-3-2 with the chords: C-E-G. In the other hand play in the spaces, that is a **One Bar Pattern**.

Syncometric Foundations = 1st and 2nd drums (primero y segundo), that's **Two Bar Patterns** like the bass below.

All About The Bass

The Herbie Hancock song Chameleon demonstrates 2 bar patterns perfectly. The bass part = drum patterns – in this case the claves, as shown below. The solo = contrary rhythmic feel, contrast.

The solo in Caribbean drums is: **Quinto** = embellishments like in Jazz. Spanish words are often used because Latin Americans know this. They know their music has African rhythms.

Brazilian Rimshot-Clave is a great foundation under solos. Play chords in the circle of fifths with the rhythm and the solos are easy to come up with, and interrelate beautifully.

From Disco to R&B, Salsa to Merengue, it is the African counter-rhythms that make the layers of "Latin Music" that is so popular. It is playing on instruments the 1st drum parts, 2nd drum, (primero and segundo) and other percussion parts becoming the embellishments beautifully interwoven.

Perpetual Motivations

A core component of the joy of making music together is having a repertoire of parts that can be played by one musician over and over, that give rhythmic and harmonic foundation so clearly defined that it is almost effortless for other musicians to hear opportune places to add phrases. These are germs – basics that germinate into full blown group motifs or collective motivations. My shortcut for these is: "Motorvations."

Cuba used to have a great musical influence over not only the United States but really the whole world. Their big bands and extravagant nightclubs are famous and well known. Much of their music allowed the African musical sensibilities to bring percussion parts into melodic music, creating repeated patterns that really add a fresh earthiness to music.

In the United States African ancestry people who were not allowed to keep their African instruments, language or culture, still brought rhythmic patterns and repeated longer motifs to the music that is now simply American music such as Jazz.

If you listen to good bass patterns in Afro-American music they act as motifs to build upon, very much like themes in classical orchestrations in symphonies, fugues and concertos.

Many African Americans will tell you that the music moves them to a place where they feel more at home. It moves them inside and in their hearts. There are amazing intrinsic ways that the African relationship with music has secretly been released in American music!

The following two scales almost magically synchronize African agogo patterns with the most common major scales. The 2 most common agogo patterns, and the 2 most common major scales!

Syncro-Nice Sacred Rhythm Scales

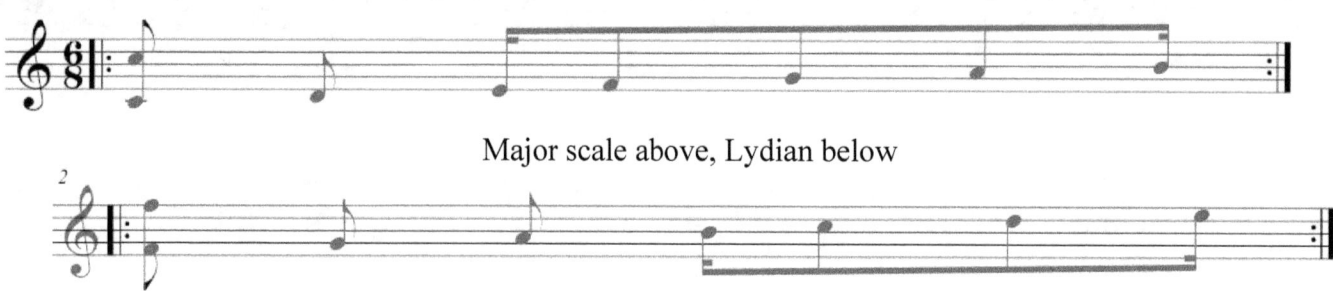

Major scale above, Lydian below

Melodic Minor

Teo Barry Vincent

Conversation Pieces Solo: 1) Chords arpeggiated 2) Scales 3) Chromatic

In general you can use the song "Heart And Soul" as a performance project because it is a recognizable well known foundation for repeatable parts that include Call and Response. It is also potent for solos – improvisation creation.

The Montuno is a Great Motorvator

The Latin Music Motorvation is the "Montuno." The Montuno defines firstly the rhythmic phrase in terms of which side it plays and it's floweriness or floriano quality (sparseness or fullness). Secondly the montuno defines the chord progression pretty fully. A complete and concise montuno will lean prominently on the leading tone from chord to chord making harmonic progression confusion impossible.

If you play a good montuno, especially with the "Tumbao" or bass pattern that is derived from African drum patterns, often it will motivate someone to start playing percussion, or even joining in with a song that they know that fits over the pattern you are playing.

If you know 5 or 10 various montuno patterns, you can be the center of a musical experience where everyone wants to join in and sing, dance, improvise, and compose complimentary parts and phrases creating collaborative new music in real time!

This type of real-time composing and improvising is one of the greatest ways that humans can act collectively to play their part and improve the whole. Again, the seeds of this type of group performance is repeated motifs of a specific design, which we are bringing to you in useful functions as Perpetual Motivators.

Montuno Etude No. 1

Dedicated to Oszkar Morzsa

2011
Teo Vincent IV

♩ = 120

That Makes This Heaven

Teo Vincent IV
(c) 2011

TIGHT SCHOOL

Here we tie a few things together smoothly by sharing with you techniques to give you enhanced overview of songs inner rhythmic phrases and arrangements. This information will help serious music artists to be able to 'get inside' the music and have clean tight chops that don't step on anyone else's part. These rules may not apply to your style or musical level but are useful rules to know. You may not play "Latin Music," but the montuno studies below can be applied to any form of music and will help you be a complementary musician and a complementing sound.

In this lesson we are reviewing and building on the rules for playing the MONTUNO - Salsa Piano part correctly depending on how the CLAVE pattern is played (the pattern for the little sticks that hold the meter, feel and pulse in Cuban music). The CHUCKS area below this one describes other ways to be on the correct side of the musical phrase as well.

Review: The Correct Side Of The Pattern

The clave pattern has definite sides. It is the most efficient way to learn the sides of musical patterns by learning clave rules. When you are talking about the sides of the pattern you are talking **percussionist rules**, or standards. For example, a part of the kinto solo in guaguanco Afro-Cuban Drumming requires that the kinto solo does not step on the clave part at all, no note of the solo can be the same as the clave's. This is a concentrated syncopation technology where the soloist not only embellishes the pattern but... tries to confuse it. I've seen cat's pull the timing two ways from sunday while a master percussionist is just trying to hold the clave pattern and it is not an easy rhythm to hold!

Tres Golpes (3 gulps or 3 pulses)

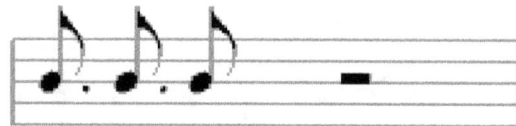

That's the first half of a clave pattern. Here you will see it in one bar and two bar charting. Jazz and Salsa is usually in CUT TIME, so the count is twice as fast. These graphics are in both types, because the percussion rules are the same.

Remember there are considered to be 2 general clave patterns, son clave and rumba clave ("Bembe Clave" is so complex, get to that later). Both of these clave's can be played in **3 - 2 or 2 - 3**, this is called the clave being on one side or the other.

3-2 SON CLAVE

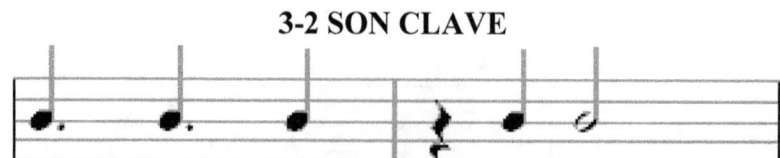

The 3 side of the clave is the down side. A 3-2 clave pattern has the down side at the beginning of the phrase instead of in the middle. The rule, and you will find it a tough one, is to never play your montuno or rhythm part on the down side of clave. The following pattern, your basic C 1 - 4 - 5 -4 montuno,

should not be played against a 3-2 clave, instead you would use one like this:

You can see that the second montuno is up on the down side of clave. You could also use a montuno where both sides are UP, and that montuno fits over any clave!

That gives you powerful concepts to think about, and years of things to practice.

CHUCKS (Accompaniment Accenting One or the Other Side)

Background and underlying rhythms are often called chucks. A good way to understand how they compliment the basic rhythmic pulse is to check out how they can be on one side of the rhythm or the other.

CHUCK ON ONE SIDE

THE OTHER SIDE (TURNED AROUND)

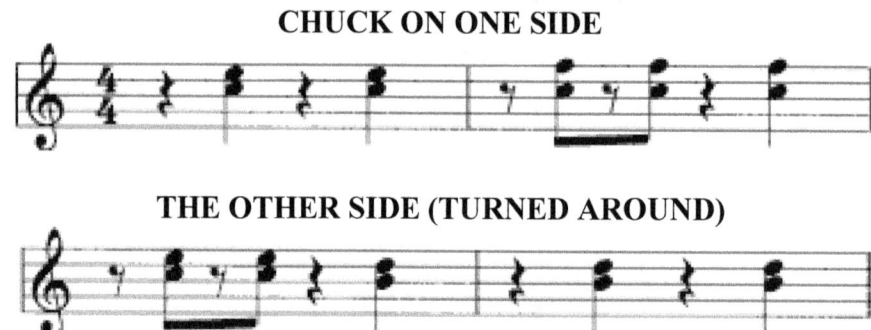

Play even just a C Major chord with these rhythms, you will see the difference in feel, and different ones (different sides) can be used in different parts of arrangements.

DESIGNING MONTUNOS

In these lessons bass parts are written in treble clef for simplicity; once you learn them take them down at least one octave. The 3 montunos above would be played over a tumbau or bass pattern like this:

C 1 - 4 - 5 - 4 TUMBAU (Bass pattern)

So put the tumbau in your left hand, then add the montuno in the right.
The following shows more bass and piano parts fundamental to montuno theory:

C TUMBAU

C7 MONTUNO 1 (or Gm7 - C7)

C7 MONTUNO 2 (or Gm7 - C7)

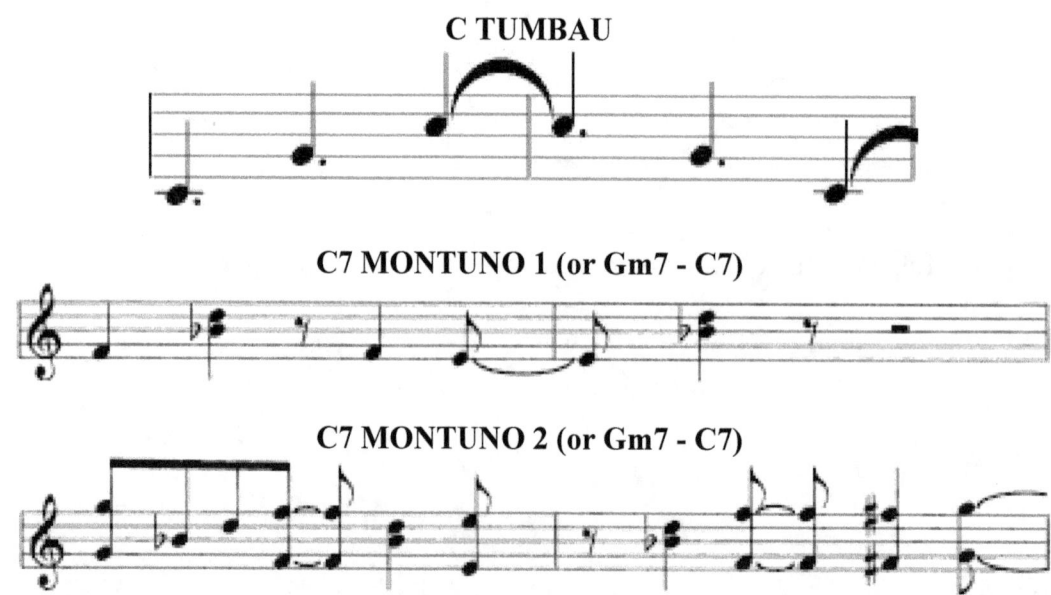

In montuno design you will find that the montuno plays a primary role in the rhythmic role of a song or progression and also a primary melodic role. When singers are getting their parts together it is often necessary for them to hear the chords, and chord progressions; often a piano or guitar is the only instrument necessary

Arboribus Musicorum *Trees of Music* • Part 4 • Page 72

for this. Montunos do all of that - show the harmonic pattern as well as the rhythmic pattern. As explained above, the montuno should be correctly layered on top of the rhythmic pulse.

To also compliment the basic melodic aspects of the song the montuno is based on the leading tones of the chords. So if the chords go from Gm to C7 the leading tones are Bb and F to Bb and E (the 3rd and 7th of both chords). You will see that that is almost exactly what C montuno 1 does above. The following example shows this even better, the leading tones in C 1 - 6 - 2 - 5 are B&E, A&E, C&F, B&F. Notice how that is exactly what the following montuno does, you could even take out the G and A on top of the piano part and it still is perfect as a montuno, defining the rhythmic arrangement and the melodic arrangement.

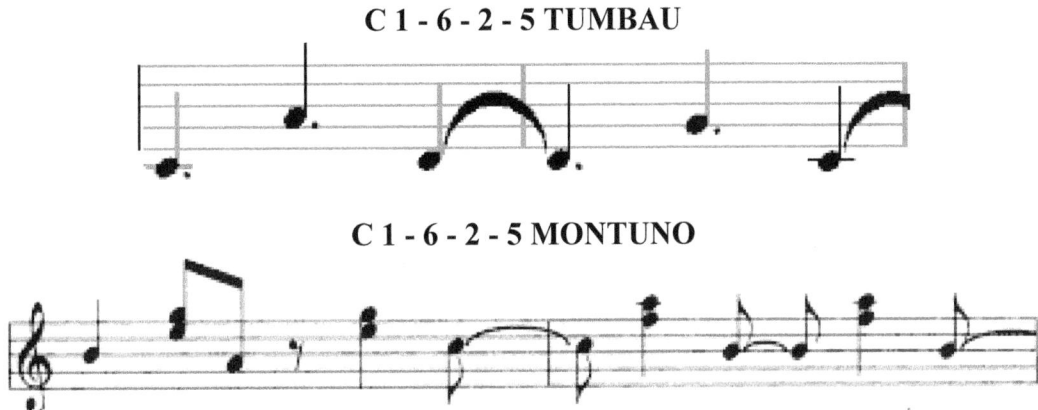

The above is a great practice for 1) circles of fifths, 2) left / right hand coordination, and 3) tumbau and montuno development. Once you can feel the delay in the montuno, against the bass hand's standard 3-3-2 timing you will be feeling and learning one of the best syncopation techniques, one syncopation leading another syncopation by just a hair! Try the above in as many keys as you can.

Calypso Guitar Chucks

In Calypso and Reggae the Motorvator is the Chuck pattern of the guitar or keyboard. It's function is the same as the montuno, defining the chordal progression and the rhythmic pattern.

One distinction between Calypso and Latin music is that in Latin percussion there is more often than not a balance of components on "one side," such as 3-2, and other components that are playing "2-3," or "opposing clave," which gives the percussionists greater and greater possibilities of interacting with various instrumental sections.

Another way to say this is that in Calypso and Reggae basically all parts will have the same chuck pattern (side).

Sections, Unions & Oppositions

Calypso Circles

2010 09 24

Teo Vincent IV

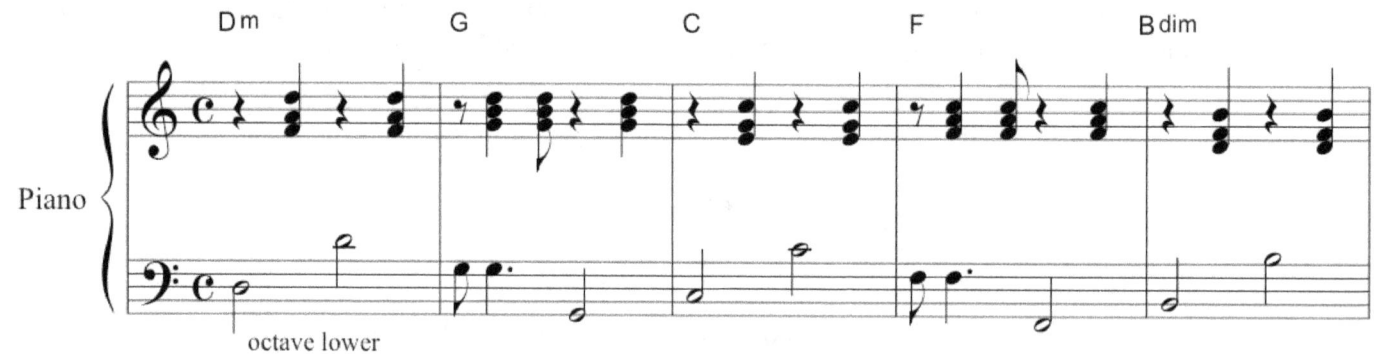

octave lower

Louisiana style Second-Line chants calls and answers

The second line in the parade has a great tradition of call-and-response from the south, southern US culture.

Give half of the group one part such as: "Shoo fly, don't bother me!"

The other half the let them answer: "Go away fly and let me be."

The first part goes again, then other answers such as: "I'm going to swat you wait and see!" It can be fun!

Another one is: "Hold 'em Joe!" answered: "No don't let 'em go." "Hold 'em Joe!" "Hold mo' and mo'!"

What we have here is the basic Call and Response common to African and other World Musics. It is also Chorus and Solo or Lead, and is really almost all that there is in Orisha songs, the sacred songs of the Nigerian Yoruba people.

The great Italian Baroque composer Antonio Vivaldi (1678-1741) used a similar concept of a group and soloist having a dialog. In *concerto grosso* there are the two: "the call," *solo* and "the answer," *tutti* (or *ripieno*) which means full in Italian.

You can hear this marvelously in his "Le Quattro Stagioni" or "The Four Seasons" where you hear wonderful dialog between the lead (solo) violinist and the orchestra (Tutti / Ripieno).

Phrases

What's the *Catch-Phrase*

In technology you need to know the buzz-words. To a fine pianist, phrasing means that the melody is to be sung, sweetly. This use of phrases is where we look at groups of instruments acting together to make pleasing and charming conversations with other groups of instruments. *"Hello, how are you today?" "Just fine! Try this trick on for size?" "That is dandy, may I join?"* And on and on.

In American music we look to the rhythm section to know if we are in 2-3 or 3-2 rhythmic phrasing. Only in advanced Latin or Jazz arrangements would we have some instruments with their clave on one side and some instruments with their clave on the other.

One of the best ways to understand the arrangement of American songs is to find out where the Clavinet part would be. This is similar to finding out where the Clave pattern would be, but it includes the rhythmic progression *and* the harmonic progression. To determine the clavinet part one need be half percussionist and half accompanist. In other musics this could be similar to the accordion part, mandolin part or cavaquino (little Brazilian guitar) part.

High Life Phrasing

That is a one or two bar rhythmic phrase arranging. In African music it goes to another level of arranging rhythmic parts translated into harmonic parts. **Nigerian Highlife** has:

1) Rhythm,
2) Line and
3) Lead Guitar (Tenor Guitar)

Parts each with their specific role.

Chord or Rhythm (Riddim in Reggae Lengua) plays chords and basic percussion phrases. The Line is a part roughly equivalent to the bassline in American songs. Repeated one or 2 bar part that fits over the Rhythm part. The Lead Guitar (often called the Tenor Guitar) plays long parts often 4 bars long, or longer, similar to the song's verse.

The Nigerian artist **King Sunny Ade** has these wonderful guitar arrangements if you can listen to his group.

Hohner D-6 Clavinet

"Soca Clav" is a good example of Soca (Soul Calypso) chuck pattern, more flowery than the rhythm guitar or piano might play, but clearly defining the harmonic and rhythmic phrase.

Soca Clav

Teo Vincent IV
(c) 2009 07 18 Givnology

A Calypsonian friend would sing "No Woman No Cry" with the 2nd section of Soca Clav above☺.

The "SuperClav" score below demonstrates a "2-3" pattern, meaning that the first half of the phrase goes "1-2-3" and the second half is the "tres gulpes" or "three gulpes" of the clave pattern. In bar 13 you hear the chords played imitating the clave like the rim-shot trap drum part in Bossanova though it is "turned around." Bossa-rimshot-clave is a central focus of much of the 1970s dance music of the United States. Try this rhythm with chords to solo with!

The bass notes give us our harmonic analysis information to determine a "i i iv v" chord progression.

Super Clavinet Technique

When you can use Motorvations:

In any type of popular music ensemble, a key to sounding good is a unified beat or pulse. How to have everyone truly feel the tempo together is a great skill for having your band sound good. You can give the motorvator to a guitarist, and have other instruments come in one at a time, finding a complimentary phrase. This "buildup" is common in soul music of good instrumentalists such as James Brown, Herbie Hancock, Kool And The Gang, Stevie Wonder, The Staple Singers, etc..

The concept of Perpetual Motivations was brought together after realizing that 1) the great Italian composer Nicolo Paganini had **Perpetual Motion** studies, and the great pianist Anton Kwerti explained a "**Motif Composing Technique**" used by Beethoven, the salami method he called it, cutting the motif into little pieces then picking them up off of the floor, figuratively. Being well grounded in Afro-Caribbean percussion concepts, montunos calypso chucks and funky soul music clavinet phrases, it all adds up to just about the same thing, with the cultural variations that are natural to any artistic analysis.

Motives, motifs and motivational inspiring

The final inspiration is the epiphany or revelation that a motif is the same as a motive as in a motivational starting point. As in looking at things for what can bring them together, cohese disparate phrases into congealable wholes. We call this: **Unidiversity**, uniting in our diversity.

The correct expression of unity allows all to find a place and way to be a part, without lessening the original idea by overdoing one's originality. A perpetual motivation is the musical equivalent to a negotiator who leaves us all with lingering positive truths stuck in our ear that remind us of the great purpose of uniting our individualities into a greater whole – greater than the sum of our parts!

Giving credit

We are grateful to artists who keep cultures alive even though they are not written down. A guitarist in Nigeria might live with his teacher and do duties for his teacher like a religious follower or devotee.

Some say that "World Music" is music that has not been written down. Some Folk Music has the same distinction. What is your opinion on the topic? Does it change just because it is written down? It certainly allows more people to play it and enjoy it. Here is a true story that illustrates this idea of writing down folk music and who should get the credit:

In many cities the most often performed Opera is "Carmen" by Georges Bizet (1838-1875). There is the famous aria (song) that Carmen sings to seduce Don José the soldier called "Carmen's Habanera." It is a masterful song, though there is an amazing history to Bizet's writing of this Habanera. We have redone it at the end of this book, adapted to teach percussion patterns with the very memorable and beautiful melody. You can also play Georges Bizet's Symphony reduction (included later in this book) to enjoy his "Eastern" composing style.

Yradier's-Bizet's-Carmen's Habanera

Can you guess where a Habanera is from? Here is one hint. In Spanish the "v" is often pronounced "b." Still can't guess? The little island of Cuba's capital city of course! Though French composer Bizet actually never went to Spain, the story goes that he composed music on a piano at the studio of Elisabeth Celeste Vernard-Chabrillan "La Mogador" (1824-1909), a writer, singer & student of Charles Gounod (1818-1893). Bizet heard her singing "El Arreglito" by Sebastien Yradier (1809-1865) *born Iradier*. (Celeste Mogador authored "The Gold Thieves" and "Memoirs of a Courtesan," the book cover pictured here, among dozens of other books and plays.)

Georges Bizet thought that El Arreglito was just an old folk melody, and ripe for the borrowing. At the last minute he found out that it actually was a published song, and then in the vocal score for his opera "Carmen," he gave credit to Sebastien Yradier. You may have heard Yradier's beautiful song "Paloma" another Habanera (often done as a Tango). Yradier learned these forms on a trip to Cuba in 1861. **So in this cross-cultural song: "Carmen's Habanera,"** Bizet was imagining a Spanish melody of a Spanish composer who was imagining Havana, Cuba, in the Caribbean, in the New World! Continuing the cultural research, Cuban music is both African and Spanish! The moral to this story is: Keep it alive, write it down. Pass it along, and you may be able to get the credit for it!

Create a Time Capsule for the Future

Music allows you to capture a feeling, document a time and place, paint a picture - sometimes better than the visual arts. Music is a language that sometimes says things that words simply can't communicate. Make your experience eternal by writing it down. Let us continue to thank those that have upheld traditions, carried on culture, language, forms and feelings that would have otherwise been neglected, and sometimes even sadly lost forever.

Be the proud upholder of traditions by writing down your wonderful songs, feelings, dances, wisdom, words and sounds. In addition, exploring the depths of emotions shared in music helps us understand our own feelings more.

Affirmatinas – Positive Message Music

Music is often employed to help remember things. It is said that Hawaiian chants will recall 20 generations of names. The song we sing to learn the A-B-C's helps remember the alphabet. It is the same song that we call Twinkle Twinkle Little Star, and early in this book we help you make your own positive affirmation song out of it.

In our section on clave patterns we showed you a positive message song phrase (in clave): **"Peace, ease and clarity – for me!"** This is a powerful positive message.

Affirmatinas

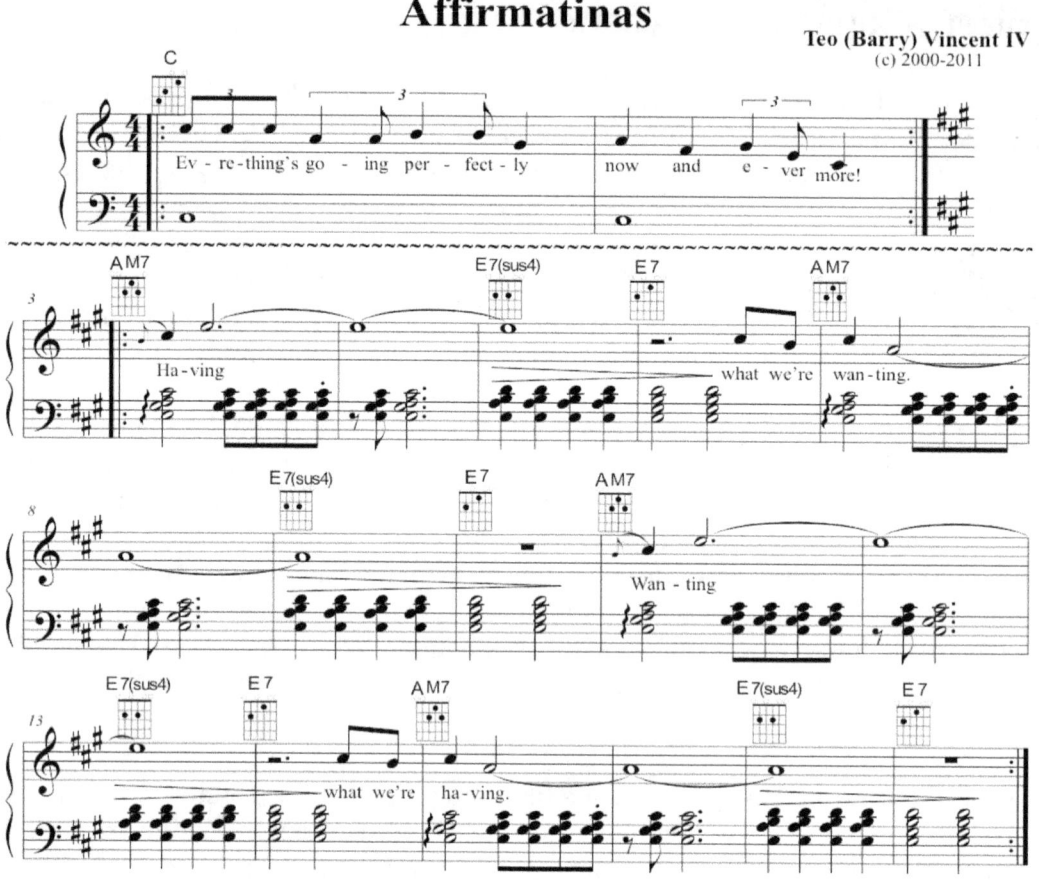

Let It Be's

ChopinMadeAWay

Chopin-Vincent

Part V: More of Vincent's Original Song's Scores

Bossanova Etude No. 1 (Lost In Love)

Teo Vincent IV
(c) 2011

Take Me Home 6

Jamming Lesson 01
(Em Circles + Handel Lines)

© 2022 0805 Teo Barry Vincent

Play [A] no line, line, solo until cued, line, other solos, the line, last time play [B] & [C].

To make this pattern easier for beginners, notice bar 5 F# minor 7 b5 b9 is simplified to "C" and the next chord, B7 b9 b13 is simplified to "Cm" in both cases it is very easy, just play C and then Cm!

The song is in E minor (which is also the key of G Major), it is the key of the Guitar, and the pattern (Circle of Fifths), is often called "Autumn Leaves chords" and is very common. This song is inspired by a Georg Handel Sonata phrase + deep moody Jazz chords but is made for fun jamming!

Guitar Jam in Mi Dominant (E7)

Guitar Jam in Mi Dominant (E7) page 2

My Fantasy

Slow Salsa Groove

Teo Barry Vincent
(c) 2011

My Fantasy 2

My Fantasy 11

Arboribus Musicorum *Trees of Music* • Part 5 • Page 104

My Fantasy 12

Lilly's Song

Theodore Barry Vincent
(2012) Teo Vincent IV

Swing Montuno Study

Allegro capriccioso - lively & playful

© 2009 09 21
Teo Vincent 4th

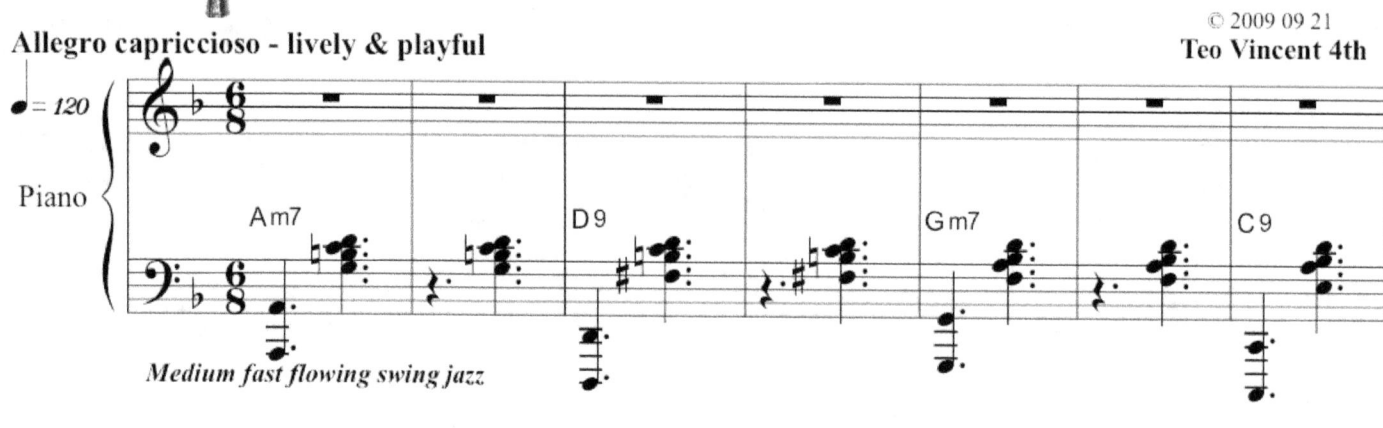

Medium fast flowing swing jazz

Swing Montuno Study (2)

Culture Crossing

Part VI: More of Vincent's Reductions & Arrangements

Arboribus Musicorum *Trees of Music* • Part 6 • Page 115

Chamber Concerto in D major, RV 93

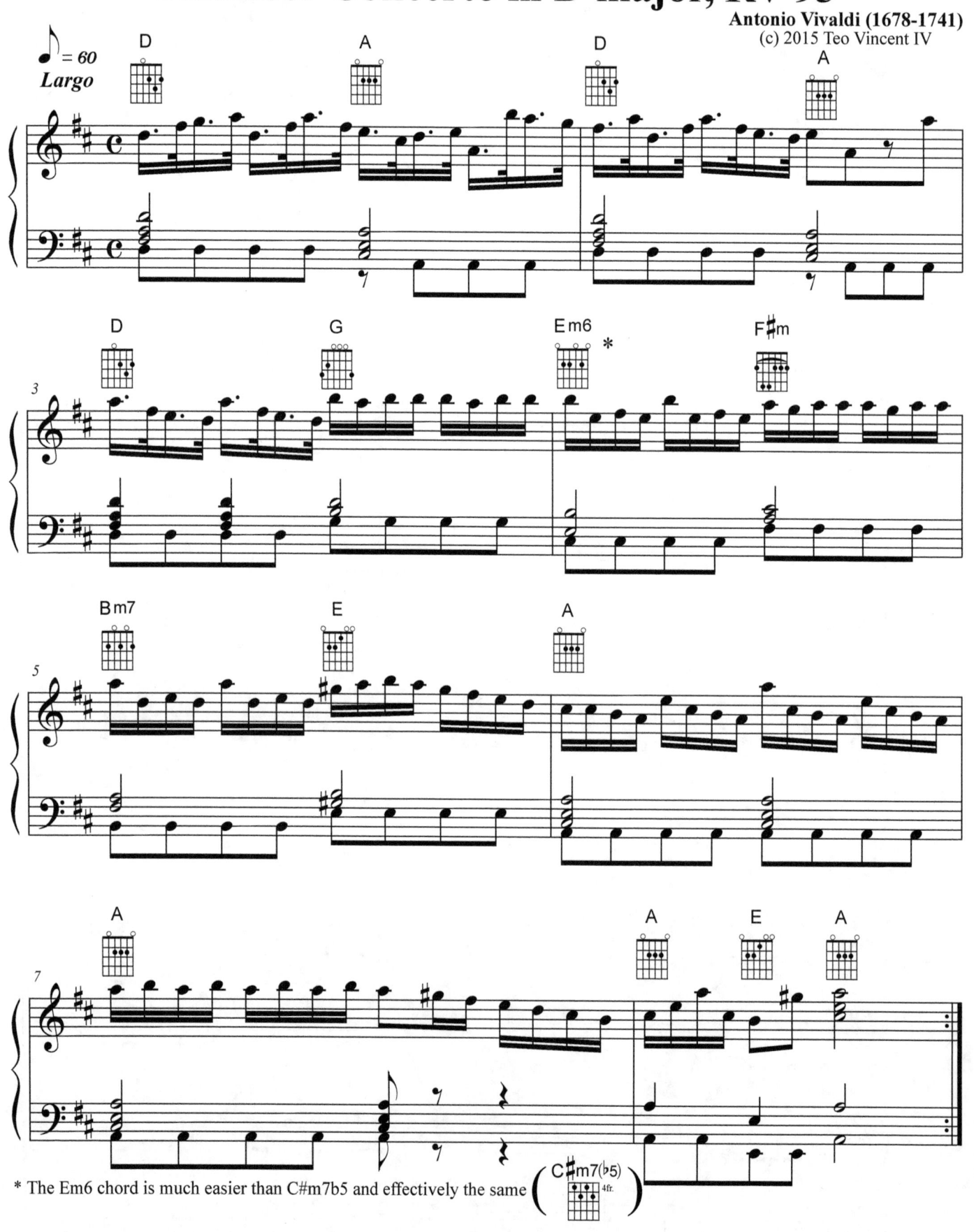

* The Em6 chord is much easier than C#m7b5 and effectively the same

Chamber Concerto in D major, RV 93 (2)

Air & Chorus "Dal tuo stellato soglio"
From the Sacred Drama "Mosè in Egitto"

Gioacchini Rossini 1792-1868
Teo Vincent IV Arranger © 2022

Air & Chorus "Dal tuo stellato soglio", p. 2

Symphony No. 88 II Largo Cantabile Largo Cantabile page 2

Cantabile

Niccolò Paganini Oct 27 1782 Genoa—May 27 1840 Nice
Teo Barry Vincent IV Finale® Score

©2023 Givnology Wellness Arts

Cantabile, p. 2

Bibliography

https://www.practicapoetica.com/articles/american-music-history-chart/
https://meaning.assurances.gov.gh/orisha-colors-and-meaning.html
The Golden Encyclopedia Of Music, Norman Lloyd, 1968 Western Publishing Company
Beyond the Romantic Spirit 1880-1922, Nancy Bachus, 2003 Alfred Publishing Co.
The Music of Man, Yehudi Menuhin and Curtis W. Davis, 1979 Menuhin Publications
The Great Pianists, Harold C. Schonberg, 1987 Simon & Schuster
The Enjoyment of Music, 11th Edition, Kristine Forney & Joseph Machlis, 2011 W. W. Norton & Company
Orin Òrìṣà, Songs for Selected Heads, John A. Mason, 1992 Yoruba Theological Archministry

About The Author

Theodore 'Teo' Barry Vincent IV is also a Developer of Wellness New Media; Programming Visionary Cultural Presentations. Designer & Inventor. First composition at age 7. Playing piano & keyboards in Soul, Jazz, Jazz Fusion, Salsa, Latin Jazz, Brazilian, Funk, Rap, African, Reggae, Calypso, Soca groups and many more! Gifted composer, singer, acoustic & electric guitarist, arranger, percussionist, improviser, Sound Designer, Multi-Keyboardist, Synthesizer Player & Solo Pianist.

By day he was a super-skilled technical writer and stand-up trainer for dozens of top Silicon Valley firms, by night playing and composing wild World Music! Now combining technical tools and classical material, rearranging and performing a wide range of styles from Romantic to Modern, Baroque to Futuristic! Amazing new orchestrations, reductions, scores and recordings. Pioneering: "Sheet Music Videos."

Technical Clients Included:

Duran, Ochoa & Icaza, LLP, La Raza Lawyers Association of the SF East Bay, The Duran Foundation, BART, Urban Families, TIS (Transaction Information Systems) Worldwide Traction Interactive Division, Inersha Sound and Communications, PMI Mortgage Insurance, Art and Education Media, The Dublin Group, The Informative Edge, Abacus, Corporate Solutions, Apple (Palo Alto, San Jose, Fremont, Cupertino, Mountain View), Claris, HP, Oracle, GreatWork, SF Mayor's Conference, SEGA, NASA, Silicon Graphics, Lawrence Livermore Laboratories, Stanford University, Stanford Research Institute, Stanford Linear Accelerator Commission, UC Berkeley, Tandem, Quantum, Adobe, Lockheed, Transamerica, Ampex, GESI, Epson, DEC, Vector Graphics, Zenith, Kaiser, Blue Cross, Pasco Scientific, Mitsubishi, Canon USA, Pacific Bell, Pacific Gas and Electric, American President Lines, Mervyns, TekLink, Beck Tech, Human Engineered Software, USI, Commodore Computer Center, Atari, Alameda County Data Processing, KQED Television, KPFA Radio.

Content may be subject to copyright. See: http://en.wikipedia.org/wiki/Fair_use
"..for purposes such as criticism, comment, news reporting, teaching, scholarship, or research.."